POLITICS is...

Senior Editor Georgina Palffy,
Designer and Illustrator Kit Lane
Senior editorial team Selina Wood,
Camilla Hallinan, Hannah Dolan, Ann Baggaley
US Editors Jenny Wilson, Lori Hand
Additional design and illustration Guy Harvey
Picture research Sarah Hopper

Managing Editor Francesca Baines
Managing Art Editor Philip Letsu
Publisher Andrew Macintyre
Art Director Karen Self
Associate Publishing Director Liz Wheeler
Publishing Director Jonathan Metcalf
Producer, Pre-Production Robert Dunn
Producer Jude Crozier

Jacket Designers Akiko Kato, Tanya Mehrotra
Jacket Design Development Manager Sophia MTT
DTP Designer Rakesh Kumar
Jackets Editorial Coordinator Priyanka Sharma
Managing Jackets Editor Saloni Singh

First American Edition, 2020
Published in the United States by DK Publishing
1450 Broadway, Suite 801, New York, NY 10018

Copyright © 2020 Dorling Kindersley Limited
DK, a Division of Penguin Random House LLC
20 21 22 23 24   10 9 8 7 6 5 4 3 2 1
001—316685—Jun/2020

A catalog record for this book
is available from the Library of Congress.
ISBN 978-1-4654-9143-5

DK books are available at special discounts when purchased in
bulk for sales promotions, premiums, fund-raising, or
educational use. For details, contact: DK Publishing Special
Markets, 1450 Broadway, Suite 801, New York, NY 10018
SpecialSales@dk.com

Printed and bound in UAE

A WORLD OF IDEAS
SEE ALL THERE IS TO KNOW
www.dk.com

POLITICS is...

WRITTEN BY
SIMON ADAMS, ELIZABETH DOWSETT, SHEILA KANANI,
ANN KRAMER, TRACEY MULLINS, PHILIP PARKER, SALLY REGAN

EDITORIAL CONSULTANT
PROFESSOR PAUL KELLY

CONTENTS

TYPES OF GOVERNMENT

POLITICAL IDEOLOGIES

POLITICS

is...

Politics is far more than the workings of government or how a state is run—it's also to do with what we as individuals believe and the kind of society we want to live in.

Most of us learn about politics first of all from our family and friends. Later, we may read or hear about current affairs online or through traditional news media. School lessons on citizenship and civics can help us understand the issues behind the news, in preparation for adult life.

However, politics is about much more than a knowledge of facts and events. It is also about our beliefs and values, and how these are represented by political parties and pressure groups. If you want to change something in the world—whether that means fighting for a local cause, such as better bicycle routes, or tackling a global issue, such as inequality—you are showing an interest in politics.

Our background, culture, or where we grow up will all have a bearing on the choices we end up making and the party we will vote for. But this is not the whole picture. Some of the most important issues of the day divide young and old. Just think of Greta Thunberg, a Swedish student challenging the most powerful world leaders because the climate emergency will dominate the lives and futures of younger people. Young people tend to be less nostalgic for the past and more hopeful for the future, too. For that reason, politicians in some countries are considering lowering the voting age—why shouldn't 16-year-olds have a voice that counts?

This book will help you make sense of your views by comparing them with political beliefs, ideas, and traditions, as well as introducing major political figures and thinkers. To defend your values or transform the world around you need to understand political systems and the complexity that underlies news stories or social media.

I hope this book will not only inform you but also challenge your ideas. Most importantly, I hope it will help you take politics seriously and use your vote well.

Professor Paul Kelly
London School of Economics
and Political Science (LSE)

WHAT IS POLITICS?

SHOULD WE ALL VOTE ON THE FOOD THAT WE WANT TO TAKE?

HOW DO WE CHOOSE THE PEOPLE WHO WILL MAKE DECISIONS?

IF SOMEONE CAN'T AFFORD THE PICNIC, SHOULD WE ALL HELP PAY FOR THEM?

HOW DO WE KNOW THE WAY? IS THERE A NAVIGATOR?

THE PEOPLE WE PICKED TO BUY FOOD ARE NOT DOING THEIR JOB. CAN WE REPLACE THEM?

HOW DO WE DECIDE WHERE TO EAT?

WHERE SHOULD WE GO FOR THE PICNIC?

SHOULD WE GET ONE PERSON TO BUY FOOD FOR EVERYONE?

Politics is not just about debates in congress or what's happening in the evening news. It's also about how decisions are made in our daily lives.

Politics is about how we organize societies, what the rules should be, and who should hold authority. On a simple level it's about how two or more people work together, overcome disagreements, and make decisions. This might involve a large group of people like a national government, or a small gathering such as your local basketball team. There are politics in everyday activities—planning a picnic, for example. For the picnic to go well, people need to agree on their aims and include as many people as possible in the decisions. It is also helpful to choose someone or some people to take charge, to set the rules, and sort out arguments. Otherwise, there may be chaos!

THERE'S NOT ENOUGH ROOM ON THE MINIBUS. DO WE TELL PEOPLE THEY CAN'T GO, OR GET ANOTHER MINIBUS?

HOW DO WE DECIDE WHO TO INVITE?

HOW SHOULD WE DECIDE WHAT FIRST AID KIT TO TAKE AND WHO SHOULD CARRY IT?

SHOULD WE HAVE A PICNIC AT ALL OR DO SOMETHING ELSE?

WHO SHOULD BE IN CHARGE OF COLLECTING MONEY FOR THE PICNIC?

SOME PEOPLE DIDN'T WANT TO BE INVOLVED IN THE DECISIONS AND NOW THEY'RE COMPLAINING ABOUT THEM. IS THAT FAIR?

HOW DO WE CATER TO PEOPLE WITH ALLERGIES?

WHAT IS POLITICS FOR?

SHOULD AIRPLANES BE ALLOWED TO TAKE OFF AT NIGHT?

WHAT IS FAIR PAY? SHOULD THE GOVERNMENT SET RULES ABOUT THIS?

BANK

SHOULD OLDER PEOPLE GET FREE BUS TRAVEL?

SHOULD THE GOVERNMENT MAKE LAWS ABOUT SAFETY AT WORK?

HOW MUCH TAX SHOULD WE HAVE TO PAY?

CRIME IS RISING IN MY AREA. DO WE NEED MORE POLICE?

SHOULD MUSEUMS GIVE FREE ENTRY?

Societies need political systems in order to run effectively. Decisions need to be made on everything from how to care for the elderly to how to cut down on crime.

We allow governments to have the authority to make these decisions. How to divide a society's resources, between funds for a police force or for education, for instance, is all a matter of politics. If we want better schools and more libraries, we may have to pay more tax to fund this, or if we want to pay less tax, we might have to cut some services. Some people prefer a government that does not make too many regulations—others welcome a lot of involvement from the state to manage society. Figuring out what our priorities are, and trying to meet the needs of as many people as possible without ignoring those of others, is one of the most important tasks of government.

Types of
GOVERNMENT

MONARCHY is...

The French Revolution

THEOCRACY is...

The Iranian Revolution

DICTATORSHIP is...

TOTALITARIANISM is...

Power on parade

OLIGARCHY is...

DEMOCRACY is...

Nelson Mandela

ANARCHISM is...

WHO'S IN CHARGE?

SHOULD PEOPLE GET TO VOTE ON EVERY DECISION?

IS IT BETTER IF ONE PERSON MAKES ALL THE RULES?

ARE SOME SYSTEMS OF GOVERNMENT BETTER THAN OTHERS?

HOW FAR SHOULD A STATE HAVE CONTROL AT THE EXPENSE OF INDIVIDUAL FREEDOMS?

CAN ELECTED REPRESENTATIVES REALLY REFLECT OUR VIEWS?

All the states of the world have governments to decide on matters such as laws, taxes, security and welfare services. But there are many types of government and people have different opinions as to which one is the best.

Throughout history, people have debated which person or group of people should take charge, whether they be tribal leaders or parliaments. Today there are three main types of government: rule by one person, who makes all the decisions; governments in which small groups are in charge; and democracies, in which a nation's citizens have the opportunity to choose a government. The type of government makes a big difference to how much freedom a country's people have in their lives. However, many of the issues that governments decide on, such as education or transportation, are similar.

SHOULD RELIGION HAVE A ROLE IN GOVERNMENT?

HOW MUCH POWER DO MONARCHS HAVE?

SHOULD THE MILITARY GOVERN THE COUNTRY?

SHOULD POWER BE INHERITED?

IS IT FAIR THAT WEALTHY ELITES HAVE POWER?

HOW EASY IS IT TO CHANGE A SYSTEM OF GOVERNMENT?

SHOULD RULERS BE CHOSEN BY THE PEOPLE?

> "The sovereign stands to his people in the same relation in which the head stands to the body."
> **FREDERICK THE GREAT (1712–1786)**
> King of Prussia

MONARCHY is...

A FORM OF GOVERNMENT IN WHICH ONE PERSON, USUALLY SELECTED BY HEREDITARY SUCCESSION, HOLDS POWER, MOST OFTEN FOR LIFE

Of all the ways of organizing government, monarchy is the oldest. There are records of monarchs going back to around 3000 BCE in Mesopotamia and Egypt. Since then, there have always been monarchs in some part of the world, although they have been known by different titles, such as pharaohs, kings, tsars, emperors, sultans, or shahs.

HEREDITARY RULE

Monarchs are normally the sole ruler of their country, although occasionally there have been joint monarchs. They generally rule until they die, although this is not always the case: in Malaysia, a new king is elected every five years. Most monarchies are hereditary: the throne passes to a family member, normally the eldest son—although in some countries a woman can become queen in her own right, not just by marrying a king. In the United Kingdom, for example, the law changed in 2011 so that if the monarch's eldest child is a girl, she can succeed to (inherit) the throne.

LIMITS ON POWER

In the purest form of monarchy, the monarch makes all the important decisions, which must be obeyed. In practice, the level of power that monarchs have exercised has varied greatly and they have not always been able to do as they chose. Roman emperors such as Augustus (ruled 27 BCE–14 CE) were supposed to consult the Senate before making important decisions.

Later, the constraints on kings became greater. In England, King John (who ruled from 1199–1216) was forced by his nobles in 1215 to sign Magna Carta, a document that placed limits on his power, such as forbidding him from arbitrarily arresting his subjects. Some monarchs objected to these controls, and in the 1600s a new

idea about kingship, known as absolutism, developed. According to this, monarchs derived their authority from God, which was known as the divine right of kings. They claimed total (absolute) power, and ruled without any legal controls. Some absolute monarchs, such as Louis XIV of France (who ruled from 1643–1715) used this power to make government more efficient, but Charles I of England (who ruled 1625–1649) became so unpopular that he was overthrown, executed, and replaced by a republic. Under this form of government, the country was ruled by parliament (a group of lawmakers) rather than a single hereditary monarch.

MONARCHY TODAY

Britain's monarchy was restored in 1660, but republicanism, the idea that monarchies should be replaced by elected rulers (or presidents), remained a strong force. It led to revolutions in America in 1776 and France in 1789, and in many other countries since then. Yet around one fifth of all countries today still have a monarch.

Most are constitutional monarchs. This means they have to rule within a legal framework known as the constitution, and respect the wishes of an elected parliament. They only have power over a very limited range of areas—for example, the British monarch has a say in the appointment of the prime minister to head the government, but in reality they choose the leader of the largest party in parliament. There are, however, still a few absolute monarchies such as Eswatini (Swaziland) and Saudi Arabia, where the king's power is unlimited.

Thinkers such as the ancient Greek philosopher Aristotle (ca. 384–322 BCE) argued that monarchy was a positive form of government, in which one person rules in the interests of the many. In contrast, he referred to a situation in which the monarch ruled badly as tyranny. Some consider that, although citizens don't get to chose their monarch, it's still a good system. As a ceremonial head of state who does not take part in politics, the monarch acts as a symbol of national unity and may be preferable to an elected president.

THE FRENCH REVOLUTION

1789–1799

At the end of the 18th century, France exploded in violence as the centuries-old monarchy was swept away almost overnight and revolutionaries rose to political power.

Before the Revolution in France, the monarch and aristocracy lived in luxury and paid no direct taxes, while ordinary people faced ruinous taxation and starved because of food shortages. The trigger for a crisis came in 1789, when King Louis XVI attempted to raise taxes further to pay the country's huge debts. Demanding fairer treatment, the oppressed people formed a National Assembly to represent the poorer classes.

On July 14, 1789, rumors that the king was to shut down the Assembly sparked riots in Paris. Mobs invaded the Bastille prison, hated symbol of royal power. In the following chaos, the Assembly took control of government, creating a new constitution.

Louis and his queen, Marie Antoinette, fled but were caught. By 1792, France was declared a republic and in 1793, the king and queen were sent to the guillotine. Many shared their fate. In a period known as the "Reign of Terror" under radical leader Maximilien Robespierre, thousands of French people were executed as enemies of the Revolution. In a reaction against his regime, Robespierre himself was overthrown and guillotined in 1794. A more moderate government lasted until Napoleon Bonaparte's rise to power in 1799.

Storming the Bastille

On July 14, 1789, a Parisian mob attacked the Bastille prison, freeing the inmates and looting weapons. The date is celebrated in France every year as Bastille Day.

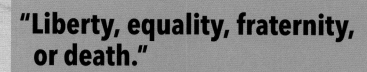

"Liberty, equality, fraternity, or death."

RALLYING CRY OF THE FRENCH REVOLUTION (1793)

"The ministry of this kingdom has been entrusted not to earthly kings but to priests."

THOMAS AQUINAS (1225-1274)
Italian philosopher and priest

THEOCRACY is...

A POLITICAL SYSTEM IN WHICH GOD, OR A SET OF GODS, ARE THE SOURCE OF POLITICAL AUTHORITY

SEE ALSO:

← Monarchy
pages 16-17

→ The Iranian Revolution
pages 22-23

In a theocracy, a ruler may claim to have been chosen by God, or a group of leaders may rule by religious laws or customs. Either way, theocratic rulers believe their right to govern is inspired by God (or a set of gods), and that right cannot be altered by normal political processes, such as democratic votes.

DIVINE RIGHT

Ruling on behalf of a god has been used to justify power in different ways. In the 17th and 18th centuries, kings in Europe claimed that their right to rule was divine, which meant that they did not have to seek permission from parliament for their actions or obey the law. In China, emperors were granted a "mandate of heaven" that gave them the right to rule. However, if an emperor ruled unjustly, he was said to have had the mandate withdrawn, giving people the right to rise up against him.

Early rulers of the Muslim world were seen as being successors (or "caliphs") to Prophet Mohammed, although arguments about the succession led to deep divisions between Sunni Muslims, who believed that the caliph should be chosen by the community, and Shia Muslims who considered it should pass through descendants of the Prophet's son-in-law Ali. Over time, the Shia developed a religious hierarchy able to make judgments based on religious law.

THEOCRATIC RULE

The nature of theocracies can vary greatly, but most have rulers who govern according to laws laid down in religious books, such as the Torah, Bible, or Koran. Iran has a parliament, but the laws it passes must be consistent with the Koran and the Supreme Leader (the head of state, who is a religious figure) can veto any laws he believes are not. In other cases, the ruler's actions are guided by religious figures, even if the country is not a theocracy. In Myanmar, the government's reaction to attacks on its minority Muslim Rohingya community has been affected by the opinions of Buddhist monks.

SECULARISM

During the Enlightenment (an intellectual movement in 18th-century Europe), the call for secularism arose, asking for religion to be taken out of the political arena. This idea was later enshrined in the US Constitution, which forbids the government from favoring a single, "established" religion. Under France's secular constitution, religious symbols are banned in schools. This separation of church and state is seen as fundamental in modern democracies. However, secularism has also been used as a means of attacking non-Christian religions. In 2011, France banned full-face veils (which some interpretations of Islam require women to wear) in public spaces, citing secularism.

RETURN TO RELIGION

Most religions have given rise to theocracies, from the Jewish kings of ancient Israel to the Christian popes of medieval Europe. Many theocracies are now consigned to history, but some do still exist. The Vatican is a modern Christian theocracy, with the Pope as head of state. The only true Islamic theocracy today is Shia Iran, where the Supreme Leader and a clerical class hold power, acting as guardians of religious law. By contrast, Sunni Saudi Arabia offers state privilege to Islam and Sharia (Islamic) law, but is ruled by a king.

In some countries, there are calls for the role of religion in the state to be restored. In Russia, the Orthodox Church (the official state religion) has become important in government affairs. There are drives in the US for religious views to be taken into account in legal matters like abortion. And in countries such as Israel and India, religious political parties have grown in influence.

THE IRANIAN REVOLUTION

1978–1979

Revolution against Iran's autocratic and pro-Western monarchy in 1979 led to the creation of the Islamic Republic of Iran. The country became a strict theocracy under clerical rule.

Iran, the modern descendant of the ancient civilization of Persia, had a long history of rule by kings. By the late 1970s, the monarchy of Shah Mohammed Reza Pahlavi—seen by many as a US puppet—was oppressive and corrupt. Opposition to the regime grew among a broad swathe of left-wing, liberal nationalist, and Islamist groups, including students and many women, until public protests and strikes forced the Shah to flee to the US in January 1979.

Ayatollah Khomeini, a leading Shia Islamic spiritual leader, returned from exile and seized control. The monarchy was abolished and in a referendum the people approved the creation of an Islamic Republic in its place. Khomeini rewrote the constitution along Islamic lines and made himself Supreme Leader for life. He died in 1989, but Iran is still ruled by a unique mix of clerics and elected politicians—though it is the unelected religious leaders who hold the power. "Un-Islamic" behavior is punished.

Unlike the Shah, Khomeini was hostile to the West. He saw the revolution as a chance to restore Iran's religious and cultural independence, after generations of Western interference. Tensions between Iran and the international community—chiefly the US and Israel—continue to this day.

Uniting the dissenters

Ayatollah Khomeini greets jubilant crowds at Tehran University in February 1979, after returning from 14 years in exile. He was seen by some Iranians as a divine figure.

"Neither East, nor West–but the Islamic Republic!"

SLOGAN OF THE ISLAMIC REPUBLIC OF IRAN

> "One does not establish a dictatorship in order to safeguard a revolution; one makes a revolution in order to establish a dictatorship."
>
> GEORGE ORWELL (1903-1950)
> British writer and journalist, writing in his novel *1984*

DICTATORSHIP is...

A POLITICAL SYSTEM IN WHICH ONE PERSON HAS POWER OVER GOVERNMENT AND DOES NOT NEED THE CONSENT OF THE PEOPLE

SEE ALSO:

→ **Totalitarianism**
pages 26-27

→ **Fascism**
pages 60-61

→ **Revolution**
pages 120-121

An authoritarian style of government, a dictatorship is formed when a country's political power is controlled by just one person: its leader, or dictator. In a dictatorship, any form of political opposition is not tolerated, and the people do not have the power to replace the dictator.

TAKING POWER
The original dictators served in the ancient Roman Republic (509 BCE–27 BCE). They were appointed in an emergency and expected to step down when it was over. Most dictators in recent history have also come to power in a time of crisis, when a political system has broken down or a revolution has happened. Many are heads of military dictatorships, meaning they originally came from the ranks of the armed forces and continue to rule with their support. For instance, Colonel Muammar al-Gaddafi's dictatorship in Libya began in 1969, when the monarchy was seen as having failed to solve the country's social and economic problems.

STAYING IN POWER
Like their ancient namesakes, modern dictators may say they will rule for a limited time, and some do step aside when the initial period of crisis is over, returning the country to democratic rule. In Spain, Francisco Franco ruled as a dictator from 1939 until his death in 1975. His successor, King Juan Carlos I, was expected to rule as a dictator, but he gradually dismantled Franco's regime and re-established democracy.

More often, they stay on until they die or are replaced by force. Some dictators, such as Robert Mugabe in Zimbabwe, are forced to step down by public protests or are overthrown by another military coup. The most powerful start virtual dynasties by passing their power to their children. In North Korea, three generations of the Kim family have ruled since 1948.

OPPRESSIVE IDEOLOGIES

Certain political ideologies have become closely associated with dictatorship. Fascism, a far-right ideology that believes in the authority of a single leader and promotes extreme nationalism, is particularly prone to it. At the other extreme, a communist government believes that it should be the sole political authority, an idea that can lead to the party's leader becoming a dictator.

IN GOVERNMENT

Although power lies with just one person in a dictatorship, the system of government may have the appearance of a democracy. There may be parliamentary elections, but in a democracy, power flows upward from the will of the people to their elected representatives who implement it, while in a dictatorship, neither people nor parliament have power. The dictator tells parliament what to do, and opposition can lead to arrest, jail, or execution. In elections, the governing party or its allies always win.

Dictators can carry out policies that may secure economic growth or political stability and they may invest in social benefits, such as education. These are known as benevolent dictators. Even then, opposition is not tolerated and people cannot replace the dictator. President Tito of the former Yugoslavia led a government that was more benign in its policies than other communist states, but he carefully managed the system to ensure no opposition could arise.

DICTATORSHIPS TODAY

Today, around 50 countries are considered to be dictatorships or authoritarian regimes (in which autocratic power is spread among more than one person). Some, like Venezuela, have slipped back from being democracies to dictatorships. Leaders of other countries, such as President Tayyip Erdoğan of Turkey, are not dictators, but have shown strong authoritarian tendencies.

> "Totalitarianism appeals to the very dangerous emotional needs of people who live in complete isolation and in fear of one another."
>
> HANNAH ARENDT (1906–1975)
> German-American political theorist

TOTALITARIANISM is...

AN EXTREME AUTHORITARIAN FORM OF GOVERNMENT THAT EXERTS TOTAL CONTROL OVER ALL ASPECTS OF PUBLIC AND PRIVATE LIFE

SEE ALSO:
← Dictatorship
pages 24–25

→ Power on parade
pages 28–29

→ Fascism
pages 60–61

Most of us have some control over our lives: how we behave, what we think, and what we do. In a totalitarian society, people do not have these freedoms. The state controls all aspects of their lives.

TOTAL CONTROL
In an authoritarian state, political power is held by a central authority at the expense of individual freedom and democracy. The authority expects and demands obedience from its citizens. Totalitarianism takes this much further. As its name suggests, a totalitarian system is one in which a state has total or absolute control over all aspects of society and its citizens. This includes control over the law, the economy, education, culture, and even behavior.

Citizens have no rights or freedom of expression, on political matters or anything else. The authority of the state is absolute, control being maintained through physical force, intimidation, thought manipulation, and mass surveillance. Opposition is not allowed. In North Korea today, Supreme Leader Kim Jong-un tightly controls every aspect of life.

POWERFUL IDEOLOGIES
Many societies in the past have been dictatorships, but the concept of totalitarianism is fairly recent. It emerged from the chaos of World War I (1914–1918), with the word first appearing in the 1920s to describe Benito Mussolini's fascist regime in Italy. Mussolini removed all political opposition by force and sought to form a totalitarian state. The word has also been used to describe Nazi Germany under Adolf Hitler's fascist government as well as the Soviet Union under communist leader Joseph Stalin, totalitarian regimes at opposite ends of the political spectrum.

This is largely due to the work of political theorist Hannah Arendt, who wrote extensively on the subject. Analyzing their regimes, Arendt pointed out that their ability to exert total control came not only from force, but also from the power of their ideologies—expressed as the inevitability of racial struggle in Nazi Germany, and class struggle in the Soviet Union—which legitimized their total control. People accepted the regimes' ideologies as ways to solve problems in their societies.

POLITICAL REPRESSION

A totalitarian state is led by a powerful dictator, ruling elite, or military leader. Elections do not take place or are carefully managed. The state wields its power through various means, including the use of terror. Secret police use torture and other forms of punishment. Any political protest or challenge to the state is put down with the utmost severity. North Korea, ruled by the Kim dynasty for three generations, is the only truly totalitarian state in the world today. Its leading political party, the Workers' Party of Korea, allows no aspect of society to be free from state control.

THOUGHT CONTROL

A totalitarian state may manipulate its citizens and try to control peoples' attitudes and thoughts. Freedom of speech does not exist, and the press is not free to express opinions. Instead, the regime controls all media, using them to broadcast only the state's aims and beliefs. It also uses propaganda to influence the views of the population in line with its ideology. The population is under constant surveillance and is aware of being watched, forcing people into obedience and ensuring that they are too frightened to do anything other than comply with the regime. It may also encourage citizens to betray others suspected of dissent. In 1949, British novelist George Orwell published *1984*, a novel that envisages a terrifying futuristic totalitarian state. The year 1984 has come and gone—but the conditions for totalitarianism still exist.

"The military might of a country represents its national strength."

KIM JONG-UN (born 1983)
Supreme Leader of North Korea

POWER ON PARADE

The Democratic People's Republic of Korea is the world's most autocratic regime, ranking last on a democracy rating of 167 countries. The totalitarian state displays its power to the world through shows of military might.

More commonly known as North Korea, the country was founded on communist ideology. After World War II (1939–1945), the Soviet Union took control of the north of the Korean Peninsula, while the US controlled the south. Soviet troops withdrew from North Korea in 1948, leaving it in the hands of the Workers' Party and its leader, Kim Il-sung.

Kim Il-sung established a personality cult around himself as Great Leader, which he consolidated by purging party officials. His son, Kim Jong-il, succeeded him and in 2011 his grandson, Kim Jong-un, took control.

Today, North Korea is the world's only truly totalitarian state. The lives of its people are closely controlled and it is largely closed to the outside world. All media serves the regime's *Juche* ("self-reliance") ideology, based on nationalism and socialism. Criticizing it can result in imprisonment and hard labor.

Isolated since the fall of the Soviet Union in 1991, the regime has plowed many of its limited resources into developing nuclear weapons to demonstrate its strength and unity. In response, the United Nations has imposed sanctions. Even relations with North Korea's closest ally and neighbor, China, have been strained. In 2018, Donald Trump was the first US president to meet with a North Korean leader—but in the following months negotiations broke down.

Regimented display
Soldiers march in unison during a highly choreographed military parade to mark the 70th anniversary of the ruling Workers' Party in Pyongyang, North Korea, in 2015.

> ## "They that are displeased with aristocracy, call it oligarchy."
> THOMAS HOBBES (1588–1679)
> English political philosopher

OLIGARCHY is...

GOVERNMENT BY A FEW PRIVILEGED PEOPLE, WHO USUALLY USE THEIR POWER IN THEIR OWN INTERESTS AND NOT THOSE OF SOCIETY

Small ruling groups who control the balance of wealth and power in a society are called oligarchies. The rule of such elite groups is similar to that of an absolute monarchy, although power is spread among several individuals rather than being held by one person.

Oligarchies were one of the most common forms of government in ancient Greek city-states. The Greek philosopher Aristotle, who first described oligarchies in the 4th century BCE, considered that they ruled in their own interests, while he called the elites who ruled in the interests of society as a whole aristocracies.

However, the distinction has not always been clear-cut. In medieval Venice, an oligarchy of merchants formed under the doge, the highest state official. Because the merchants had made the city wealthy for all, they felt that they should control it. In Britain, until the 1800s, most politicians came from a small number of rich, influential families. They thought of themselves as an aristocracy, ruling for the good of all, though the many poor people denied a decent standard of living might not have agreed.

MONEY AND CONNECTIONS
Family connections often determine who belongs to an oligarchy. Rulers hand down control to the next generation, and outsiders have little chance of entering the privileged circle. This is what we now understand as aristocracy. Common in the past, especially in Europe where the upper classes monopolized power for centuries, aristocratic influence is rarer now. However, even in a full democracy, small family groups can dominate, providing political leaders. Possession of a great deal

of money can be enough to hand newcomers a share of power. After the fall of the Soviet Union in 1991, a class of "oligarchs" emerged in Russia whose control of wealth meant they could dictate government policy. This kind of system is also known as a plutocracy, and elements of it can be found wherever those with money exercise an undue influence on the government.

The form of oligarchy most likely to benefit society is meritocracy, or rule by those selected because of ability. One example is the Chinese Confucian bureaucracy, which governed Imperial China for more than a thousand years until the early 1900s. Entry into government was by competitive examinations, so only the educated had a chance of success.

WHO LEADS AN OLIGARCHY?

In modern oligarchies, there may be a nominal president or prime minister, but this person's actions are dictated by the group to suit its own interests. Sometimes, the head of government is also an oligarch. At other times, as in Russia, political leaders must take into account the interests of groups who compete for a share of power, including those in the military and intelligence services. In some oligarchies, the members may adopt political labels, such as socialist, liberal, or conservative, but these are really for their own convenience. When communist regimes fell in Eastern Europe after 1989, oligarchs who had held power in the Communist Party simply transferred their role to a new political party.

WHOSE INTERESTS?

By definition, an oligarchy governs in its own interests. However, oligarchies want long-term power, so they need their societies to remain stable and prosperous. With this in mind, they may make concessions to those who are not part of the elite, or offer entry into the group to others as a means of reducing opposition. They may also promote policies leading to economic growth. Outsiders who try to take power from the oligarchy, however, are strongly opposed.

> "Government of the people, by the people,
> for the people."
>
> ABRAHAM LINCOLN (1809–1865)
> 16th president of the United States

DEMOCRACY is...

GOVERNMENT BY THE PEOPLE, EITHER DIRECTLY OR THROUGH ELECTED REPRESENTATIVES WHO GOVERN ON BEHALF OF THE PEOPLE

SEE ALSO:

→ **A constitution**
pages 72–73

→ **Suffrage**
pages 88–89

→ **An election**
pages 84–85

A democracy is a system of government that gives people the power to choose who they want to lead them and govern the country. The term "democracy" comes from two Greek words *demos* (people) and *kratia* (power or rule), and it was Athens in ancient Greece that developed the earliest form of democracy, in the 6th century BCE.

TYPES OF DEMOCRACY

The majority of countries today are democracies, but they are not all the same. The earliest examples, such as in Athens, were direct democracies. People attended debates, known as assemblies, and cast votes on issues of the day.

As countries grew bigger and their populations increased, gathering everyone to vote in person, in one place, on every issue became impractical. Instead, representative democracy developed, which is now the norm. In a representative democracy, people vote for representatives who then make decisions on their behalf for a fixed time, or term of office, in an assembly or parliament.

Today, direct democracy survives in referendums, where a government asks its citizens to vote on a specific question. Some countries do this only once or twice in a generation, on issues of historic importance, such as the United Kingdom's 2016 "Brexit" vote on whether to leave the European Union. Others, such as Switzerland, hold several referendums a year, as a regular part of the process of government, to give citizens the final say in agreeing key new policies.

IMPERFECT DEMOCRACY

A democratic government only has authority if it gains the consent of the people, through elections of some kind—but what exactly does "the people" mean? In ancient Athens, only free male citizens over the age of 20 whose parents were both Athenian were allowed to vote—women, slaves, and foreigners living in Athens were excluded, even though they made up 80–90 percent of the population. Modern democracy relies on "universal suffrage," where every citizen has the right to vote, regardless of their gender, race, wealth, or status. In reality, however, some democracies fall short of this ideal, by limiting who can stand for election and who can vote, or by manipulating how the votes are counted.

Even a fully functioning democracy isn't perfect. Every election has winners and losers, and people who have voted for the losing side may feel they are being ignored. The Greek philosopher Aristotle (384–322 BCE) argued that in a country where the poor vastly outnumbered the wealthy, educated elite, democracy could degenerate into rule by the crowd, or "mob rule." Instead, Aristotle favored rule by a single, wise monarch.

Some also worry that democracy fosters "short-termism"—if elections are held every four or five years, politicians may make popular decisions to get themselves re-elected, but these may not be for the long-term good of the country.

However, it is generally agreed that spreading power among the people and limiting a leader's term of office is not only fair, but reduces the risk that a single person will make bad decisions.

DEMOCRATIC FREEDOMS

Modern democracy can only function if people are free to make an informed choice in elections. Today's governments have more power than ever to control the news people receive through the internet and social media. A secure legal framework and a free press, in which issues can be debated, are vital to a well-functioning democratic society.

Nelson Mandela

1918–2013

Activist and politician Nelson Mandela fought for the civil rights of the people of South Africa. By challenging his country's apartheid system, a racial divide that discriminated against nonwhite people, he brought an end to segregation. Mandela ushered in a new era of democracy that gave every citizen the right to vote, regardless of the color of their skin.

> **"Real leaders must be ready to sacrifice all for the freedom of their people."**

Early activism

Born in South Africa in 1918, Mandela was the first of his family to go to school. He later went on to college, training as a lawyer in Johannesburg. It was there that Mandela met activists who were part of the African National Congress (ANC), a political group fighting for the rights of black Africans. Mandela became a leader of its Youth League in 1944.

Fighting apartheid

In 1952, Mandela led nonviolent protests against South Africa's "pass" laws, which forced nonwhite citizens to carry passes in "white-only" public places. This was part of South Africa's brutal apartheid ("apartness") system, introduced by the ruling National Party in 1948. Apartheid forced white and nonwhite people to live in separate areas and use different public facilities. Nonwhites were also denied the right to vote. Deciding nonviolent protests were not enough, Mandela helped to found *Umkhonto we Sizwe* ("Spear of the Nation"), the military wing of the ANC. In 1964, Mandela was tried as a terrorist and sentenced to life in prison.

Democratic leader

Mandela's 27 years behind bars, mostly on Robben Island, made him a global symbol of the fight for racial equality, and his name became a rallying cry for black South Africans. In 1989, amid international pressure, the South African government began talks with Mandela, and he was set free in 1990. Elected president of the ANC, he worked with the government toward a nonracial democracy. In 1994, in the first election in South Africa in which all races voted, the ANC won and Mandela became the country's first black president.

Racial unity
When South Africa hosted the Rugby World Cup in 1995, Mandela asked all races to support the national team, the Springboks. He shook the captain's hand to show racial unity. An international boycott of the all-white team had helped end the apartheid system.

Advocate for peace
Mandela won the Nobel Peace Prize in 1993 for his work in South Africa. He retired as the country's president in 1999, but continued to fight for peace and social justice around the world.

"Anarchism is the great liberator of man from the phantoms that have held him captive."

EMMA GOLDMAN (1869–1940)
Lithuanian–American anarchist and political activist

ANARCHISM is...

THE BELIEF THAT GOVERNMENT ITSELF IS WRONG, AND THAT SOCIETY WOULD BE BETTER OFF IF IT IS ABOLISHED ENTIRELY OR IN PART

SEE ALSO:

Anarchists believe that it is possible to have a society in which rules are not imposed from above, and that the way society organizes itself can come voluntarily from the people. Anarchism is not the same as anarchy, which is what happens when respect for rules and order is completely done away with. So while anarchy may occur when people rise up against the power of the state, anarchists believe that—once state power has been abolished—the people are able to cooperate to make life fairer and more equal without the state controlling them.

ANTI-AUTHORITY

Most anarchists believe that people are essentially good and the state has corrupted them over time. They see government as inherently wrong because it organizes society in the interests of a small number of people. Many anarchists also believe that people are capable of willingly working together to produce what they need, and that small groups such as communes are the best way to organize society, empowering individuals to form their own networks, They typically reject the way capitalist societies have developed, so anarchists are often politically left-wing. However, their distrust of the state as well as rejection of taxes or controls on the rights of the individual, such as the right to bear arms, means there are right-wing anarchists, too. These include militia groups in the US.

DESTROYING THE STATE

Anarchists' main political aim is to destroy the state. During the Russian Revolution in 1917, some people believed that they were achieving this and that the state, as the German political theorist Friedrich Engels said, would simply "wither away." Although the Revolution brought about sweeping changes in the structure of Russian society, a new kind of government ultimately replaced the old one. The paradox of anarchism is that opposition to any form of state puts power beyond its grasp.

In Spain, anarchist ideas took hold across many parts of society in the years before the Spanish Civil War (1936–1939). Small anarchist groups sprung up in the countryside, proposing peasant communes, while others advocated "propaganda of the deed"—local acts of revolt. Workers adopted a variant of anarchism called anarcho-syndicalism, which aimed to destroy capitalism through the working-class power of trade unions. In 1936, anarchist revolutionaries controlled much of Republican Spain, but failed to overthrow the government in favor of a workers' state—arguing that this would create an anarchist dictatorship, and a dictatorship could never be anarchist.

IN ACTION

Although anarchists tend to reject the state, unless they are fully self-sufficient they cannot operate without it. There are, however, examples of anarchist networks and communities that function well on a smaller scale. One example is the kibbutz movement in Israel, where all residents work together and contribute to the commune. Anarchist ideas have been adopted by other political causes, too, such as the student protests of the 1960s, the progressive anti-globalization movement Occupy in the early 2010s and, more recently, the environmental movement Extinction Rebellion. Anarchists also point to the informal self-help networks that spring up to provide critical resources after disasters, such as Hurricane Katrina (which struck New Orleans, Louisiana in 2005), as a sign that what they propose is a more natural form of society than a government.

Political
IDEOLOGIES

SOCIALISM is...

Karl Marx

COMMUNISM is...

Tiananmen Square

LIBERALISM is...

CAPITALISM is...

Fall of the Berlin Wall

NEOLIBERALISM is...

CONSERVATISM is...

FASCISM is...

Hitler's rise to power

POPULISM is...

The election of Donald Trump

WHAT'S THE BIG IDEA?

COOPERATION RATHER THAN COMPETITION

A MIXED ECONOMY OF PRIVATE BUSINESSES AND STATE WELFARE

LIBERALS THINK THAT EVERYONE HAS THE RIGHT TO PURSUE THEIR OWN GOALS

SOCIALISTS BELIEVE THAT SERVICES SUCH AS HEALTHCARE SHOULD BE STATE-OWNED

EQUAL RIGHTS FOR ALL PEOPLE, REGARDLESS OF GENDER, RACE, OR RELIGION

EVERYONE CONTRIBUTES TO AND SHARES THE BENEFITS OF THE STATE EQUALLY

COMMUNISTS BELIEVE IN A CLASSLESS SOCIETY, REGULATED BY IDEOLOGY

We all have our own idea about what makes a good society. We may have a view on what is a fair wage, or how old someone should be to drive, for instance.

Politicians and governments are often motivated by sets of beliefs, or ideologies, about the best way to organize society and who should have authority. To help people understand the differences between these beliefs, they can be plotted on a spectrum ranging from left to right. Beliefs that are on the opposite end of the spectrum have opposing views. The ideologies on the left, such as communism and socialism, are associated with social equality and opposition to rigid hierarchies. Those on the right, such as conservatism, stand for social order and private ownership. Liberalism, in the middle, calls for individual freedoms and mixed economies.

PEOPLE SHOULD BE ABLE TO MAKE A PROFIT AND BENEFIT FROM THE FREE MARKET

CONSERVATIVES BELIEVE IN STABILITY, PRIVATE PROPERTY, AND PRACTICAL SOLUTIONS

COMPETITION IS NECESSARY FOR SOCIETY TO PROGRESS

EVERYONE HAS A NATURAL PLACE IN SOCIETY—HIGH OR LOW

PEOPLE ARE BETTER OFF TAKING CARE OF THEMSELVES

HERITAGE, AUTHORITY, AND DUTY ARE KEY TO A SOCIETY'S STABILITY

FASCISTS BELIEVE THAT THE STATE SHOULD HAVE TOTAL CONTROL

> # "For me, socialism has always been about liberty and solidarity."
> JACQUES DELORS (born 1925)
> French and European politician

SOCIALISM is...

THE BELIEF THAT PEOPLE IN A SOCIETY SHOULD SHARE A COUNTRY'S WEALTH EQUALLY

SEE ALSO:

→ **Communism**
pages 46–47

→ **Karl Marx**
pages 44–45

→ **Capitalism**
pages 52–53

→ **Neoliberalism**
pages 56–57

Since the global economic downturn triggered by the financial crisis of 2008, there has been a renewed interest in socialism as an alternative to free-market capitalism. Based on ideas of social justice, common ownership, and cooperation rather than competition, socialism sits on the left of the political spectrum. The color red, and in particular a red rose, is a symbol of socialism, representing the blood of workers struggling against capitalism.

STATE OWNERSHIP
Socialists believe that the means of producing goods and services, such as factories and infrastructures, should be publicly owned, either by the state or some form of workers' control. What is produced should be distributed equally, according to need. The state should fund the necessities of life, such as schools, health provision, and housing, which should be paid for through taxes.

SOCIAL UPHEAVAL
Socialism emerged in the early 19th century as a reaction against capitalism and the upheavals of the Industrial Revolution. The German philosopher and economist Karl Marx saw socialism as an essential step on the way to communism, the abolition of private property, and the creation of a classless society. Some early socialists, often described as "utopian," set up cooperatives and experimented with communal living. Others fought to achieve socialism through trade unions (worker associations that act to protect workers' rights) or through revolutionary movements, such as the Paris Commune, which took control of Paris, France, for two months in 1871. Socialism went on to become a powerful political force in many nations.

DEMOCRATIC SOCIALISM

Democratic socialists seek to achieve socialism gradually rather than by revolution. They believe that a democratically elected government should regulate the economy and public services. Healthcare and education should be free, funded through taxes, and pensions and welfare benefits should be available to all. Public services and industries, such as transportation, should be publicly owned rather than run for private profit. With the exception of small businesses and homes, democratic socialists seek to extend public ownership to all property. One example of a democratic socialist government was that of the UK's Labour Party in 1945. It established the National Health Service, the first free healthcare system in the world. More recently, politicians such as Bernie Sanders of the Democratic Party have described themselves as democratic socialists and pushed for socialist programs.

SOCIAL DEMOCRATS

Unlike most socialists, social democrats accept capitalism, arguing that it can be reformed. They favor a mixed economy of privately and publicly owned business and state-funded welfare to eradicate poverty. Social democratic parties exist in most European countries and have been elected to government, most notably in the Nordic countries (Denmark, Iceland, Finland, Norway, and Sweden). The so-called "Nordic model" merges socialist principles with capitalism, maintaining private ownership but enabling trade union bargaining to achieve better conditions for workers and funding a comprehensive welfare state.

REVOLUTIONARY SOCIALISM

At the other end of the spectrum, many socialists believe that socialism will never be achieved through the ballot box. They think that capitalist ideology and practice are so deeply embedded and vested interests are so powerful that revolution is the only way to achieve a socialist society. Socialist revolutions have taken place in the past, notably in Russia in 1917, where revolution was based on so-called Marxist-Leninist principles and its aim was to set up a communist state.

Karl Marx

1818–1883

Karl Marx was a revolutionary socialist and philosopher who predicted a future in which workers would overthrow capitalism and build a communist society where all were equals. Marx never lived to see his beliefs put into action, but his ideas went on to shake up politics in the 1900s. His prolific writings have had a powerful influence on political movements around the world.

> "The workers have nothing to lose but their chains. Workers of the world, unite!"

Political scholar

Born in 1818 in Trier in Prussia (now Germany), Karl Marx studied law and philosophy. His work as an academic and a journalist gave him insight into political and social issues and led him to believe that economics was key to improving society's ills. He was also influenced by the early 19th-century German philosopher Georg Hegel, who wrote that tensions in society would lead to progress.

Radical writer

In 1843, Marx moved to Paris. Europe was then seething with radical political ideas, and to many people seemed ripe for revolution. In Paris, Marx renewed an old friendship with fellow German philosopher Friedrich Engels, with whom he collaborated on his most famous texts. In 1848, they published their influential pamphlet, *The Communist Manifesto*, which predicted the overthrow of capitalism and the creation of a communist society. They agreed that the working classes worldwide were a potential force for revolution and change. His political ideas made Marx unwelcome in Europe. Forced into exile, he moved to London in. Here, he wrote *Das Kapital* (1867), which examines the nature of capitalism and its exploitation of workers who fail to profit from the system.

Legacy

Marx's views on class conflict were interpreted as proof that communism would replace capitalism. His beliefs, under the label of Marxism, were taken up by revolutionary movements and became the party line in countries including the Soviet Union, China, and Cuba. What Marx would have thought of the actions carried out in his name we do not know.

Personality cult
Marx's name and image were glorified in the Soviet Union, alongside those of the first Soviet head of government, Lenin (above right). The Soviet Union, a communist state established in 1922, was run along Marxist–Leninist principles.

Political capital
Marx has become a political icon, but his work did not earn him much of a living. His mother said, "If only Karl had made capital, instead of just writing about it." Engels helped to support Marx, but when Marx died, he was penniless.

> ## "From each according to his ability, to each according to his needs."
> KARL MARX (1818–1883)
> Revolutionary thinker, philosopher, and economist

COMMUNISM is...

A POLITICAL PHILOSOPHY THAT SEEKS TO ESTABLISH COLLECTIVE OWNERSHIP AND CREATE AN EQUAL SOCIETY

Followers of communism, who are known as "communists" want to create a society built on social justice, equality, and cooperation. In particular, they seek to abolish private ownership of all kinds and replace it with a system of collective ownership in which all things in society are owned equally. In such a system, each person works for the good of society according to his or her ability, and each shares in the benefits according to need.

Communism sits on the far left of the political spectrum. It is similar to socialism, with its emphasis on social justice and cooperation, but communism goes further as it aims to abolish private ownership completely and create a classless society.

ANTI-CAPITALISM
Communists aspire to overthrow the economic system of capitalism, which they argue produces a great division between rich and poor. They believe that the structures of capitalism and industrialization create a privileged class, the bourgeoisie, who own the means of production (factories, shops, businesses, and services), and the proletariat (working class) who produce goods and are exploited and kept in poverty.

MARXISM
In 1848, Karl Marx, together with fellow German philosopher Friedrich Engels, published *The Communist Manifesto*. In this document, Marx outlined the route to communism. He argued that capitalism not only exploited people but it would also destroy itself because it created financial instability and tension between classes in society. He believed that class struggle

would initially lead to socialism and later, inevitably, to communism—a classless, stateless society based on common ownership. Marx's principles remain the basis of communist ideology today.

REVOLUTION

In the early 1900s, socialism and communism were attractive ideologies for those who opposed capitalism. A number of countries sought to establish communist systems. In Russia in 1917, Lenin and the Bolsheviks led industrial workers into a communist revolution to overthrow the Tsar (Russia's absolute ruler). It was at this time that the communist symbol—the hammer (representing industrial workers) and the sickle (signifying peasants)—was first adopted. From 1922, Russia and neighboring regions were incorporated into a large federal nation, the Soviet Union. Under Lenin, and from 1924 Joseph Stalin, it was run on what became known as "Marxist-Leninist" principles. A central authority, the Communist Party, was formed to represent workers and peasants. Private ownership was ended but instead of introducing common ownership, the state owned and ran the economy. In theory the Party ran the Soviet Union for the good of the people; in practice the Soviet Union, particularly under Stalin, became a single-party dictatorship.

COMMUNIST STATES

In 1949, China adopted a form of communism, known as "Maoism." It differed from Marxism-Leninism in that agricultural workers rather than industrial workers were the main drivers of the revolution. The Chinese Communist Party was a central authority that ruled China. Other countries that adopted communist-style regimes were Cuba, Vietnam, and North Korea.

ACHIEVING COMMUNISM

Some argue that neither Stalin's Soviet Union nor Mao's China were communist. Instead, they were authoritarian regimes, in which people lost their freedoms. This was not Marx's view of communism. In the years after the fall of the Berlin Wall in 1989, communism as a political ideology fell out of favor, but since the 2008 global financial crash and its impact on people's lives, there has been a renewed interest in its ideas.

"They are exchanging our economic freedom with our political freedom."

WU'ER KAIXI (born 1968)
Student protest leader

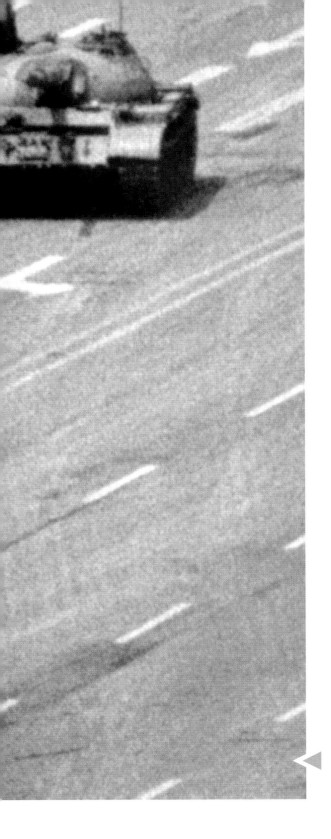

TIANANMEN SQUARE

JUNE 4, 1989

In 1989, months of peaceful pro-democracy and anti-corruption protests in Tiananmen Square, Beijing, culminated in an extreme response by China's communist rulers.

The 1980s was a time of change for China, following the death of its leader Mao Zedong in 1976. Mao's Chinese Communist Party (CCP) had taken control in 1949. Influenced by Marxism, Mao created his own Chinese form of communism, known as Maoism.

Mao's 1958 Great Leap Forward, a drive to transform industry and agriculture, had caused harsh labor conditions and famine, killing tens of millions of people. The 1966 Cultural Revolution, a brutal crackdown on perceived anti-communist behavior, also resulted in millions more deaths.

The 1980s brought economic reform to China, but also corruption. In April 1989, student protesters gathered in Tiananmen Square, calling for greater political freedom. In May, the government sent the military to Beijing to break up the crowds, which now numbered up to a million people, but the protestors were unmoved. On June 3, tanks rolled into the square. The next day, soldiers fired on the crowd, killing thousands. In the aftermath, many more were arrested.

Today, China is a global economic power, combining Mao's communism with a form of state-controlled capitalism. Dissent is not tolerated and the events in Tiananmen Square are a forbidden subject.

Tank man
The image of an unknown, unarmed man barring the path of a tank became a symbol of defiance around the world, but not in China.

"Classical liberalism is the idea that individual freedom and limited government are the best way for humans to form a free society."

DAVE RUBIN (born 1976)
American political commentator

LIBERALISM is...

A POLITICAL PHILOSOPHY THAT PLACES THE RIGHTS AND FREEDOMS OF THE INDIVIDUAL AT THE HEART OF POLITICS

SEE ALSO:

Freedom of speech, a free press, and equal rights are just some of the values associated with liberalism. The word "liberalism" comes from the Latin *liber*, which means "free." Liberalism is a broad concept that includes both economic and political ideas. Economically it supports free trade and small government. Politically it identifies with social reform and human rights, and in the US the term "liberalism" is associated by some with socialism. Liberal principles have formed the basis of Western liberal democracy and its emphasis on democratically elected governments.

ENLIGHTENED THINKING

Liberalism sits in the center of the political spectrum, except in the US, where it is seen as left wing. Its roots lie in the 17th and 18th centuries, when thinkers questioned the idea of divine rights granted by God. Arguing that humans are born with natural rights, they challenged the authority of monarchy and church. John Locke, a 17th-century English liberal philosopher, argued for a "social contract" between citizens and government. Two centuries later, English theorist John Stuart Mill expanded on this. In what is known as classical liberalism, Mill argued that individuals should have the opportunity to live as they wish, provided they do not harm others. The role of governments should be to introduce laws that enable and protect these freedoms.

LIBERAL ECONOMICS

Historically, liberals have tended to support capitalism. They believe in government intervention for social issues but limited government interference economically. The 18th-century Scottish liberal economist Adam Smith was the first to argue for free trade, believing that the market would adjust itself naturally, according to the laws of supply and demand. This belief dominated liberal thinking until the economic downturn known as the Great Depression in the 1930s, when British liberal economist John Maynard Keynes argued that during times of hardship governments should intervene to support economies and introduce welfare measures.

A REFORMING INFLUENCE

Liberalism has been a powerful political and reforming force. Its ideas of liberty and individual rights influenced the American Revolution of 1776 and the French Revolution of 1789, helping to shape modern democracy. Its influence continued throughout the 19th and 20th centuries, finding expression in liberal political parties and governments. In the present day, liberals support social reform, such as women's, gay, and disability rights as well as freedom of speech and religion. Yet liberalism has been challenged by socialism, conservatism and, most recently, the rise of neoliberal economics. It is a less powerful political movement than it was.

LIBERTARIANISM

In some ways, libertarianism is an extreme form of liberalism. Libertarians place personal liberty above all else. They argue that the individual should be free to do exactly as they wish, without government intrusion, especially with regard to free-market trading. Libertarians are found in both right- and left- wing political movements. On the left, they include some anarchist groups that believe that any form of state is harmful. On the right they have included the Tea Party movement, which is anti-taxation and supports an extreme free market.

"Capitalism delivers the goods."
LUDWIG VON MISES (1881–1973)
Austrian economist, historian, and sociologist

CAPITALISM is...

AN ECONOMIC SYSTEM IN WHICH A COUNTRY'S TRADE AND INDUSTRY ARE PRIVATELY OWNED AND RUN FOR PROFIT

SEE ALSO:

← **Communism**
pages 46–47

← **Liberalism**
pages 50–51

→ **Neoliberalism**
pages 56–57

→ **Globalization**
pages 142–143

Associated with big business and banks, capitalism supports private ownership, competitive markets, and wealth creation. As a political ideology, capitalism sits on the right of the political spectrum. Supporters of capitalism are called "capitalists."

OWNERS AND WORKERS
Capitalism influences politics because it promotes a particular view of how society should be organized. Capitalists believe that industries, including financial services, should be privately owned, whether by an individual or a huge corporation (large company or group of companies) and should be run to make profits. In a capitalist country, such as the US and those in Europe, companies employ people or a workforce, who are paid wages. Workers usually have no share in the businesses—profits go to the owners or to shareholders (people who own shares in a company), or other companies who have a stake in the businesses. Government intervention in business is limited.

AN INVISIBLE HAND
Modern capitalism has its roots in the industrialization of the 18th and 19th centuries. In his book *The Wealth of Nations* (1776), the Scottish economist Adam Smith promoted the idea of a trading market that was relatively unregulated by government. He believed such markets stabilize without state intervention because the law of supply and demand, which he called "an invisible hand," automatically regulates the market. According to this law, competition between suppliers is good because it pushes prices down; scarcity of goods pushes prices up. Smith thought that the market should determine wages and workers' conditions. He

also believed that most people operate from logical self-interest; it is in a person's interest to work hard because that is how he or she will gain rewards.

CAPITALISM TODAY
Today, many of the world's economies are based on the capitalist system, although some adjustments have been made. Countries, such as Iceland and Sweden, have what is known as a "mixed economy"—part of their economies are left to the free market while their governments manage areas such as health and transportation. Other nations, such as the US, have adopted neoliberalism, a political policy in which unregulated trade forms a central part. Most capitalist governments impose some trading standards on items such as food, and many capitalist countries have introduced minimum wages for employees.

FREEDOM OF CHOICE
Supporters of capitalism argue it has brought great benefits—it has created jobs, improved people's lives, and enabled many to own their own homes. Competition between suppliers has encouraged innovation in a vast range of consumer goods. Many people claim that capitalism creates freedom of choice and opportunities for individuals to gain from society. However, this is not always the case. China, for instance, operates a system known as "state capitalism," in which the state controls all aspects of industry and trade. Personal freedom and civil liberties are extremely limited.

SHARP DIVISIONS
Critics of capitalism argue that it is unjust and that it concentrates wealth in the hands of a small group of people, leaving others less well off or in poverty. It can exploit working people by providing inadequate wages, or cause them to lose their jobs if a market collapses. With its constant drive for increased productivity and economic growth, capitalism is also seen as responsible for using up natural resources and driving the climate emergency.

FALL OF THE BERLIN WALL

November 1989

When the Berlin Wall fell in 1989, the event was more than the demolition of a concrete border. It also marked the symbolic end of the Cold War, a 40-year period of political conflict between East and West.

After World War II, Germany was divided in two by the Allies. In 1949, West Germany became a capitalist democracy with strong ties to Western countries, while East Germany came under the control of the communist Soviet Union. The German capital, Berlin, was split between both countries.

After the division, the lives of East Germans were restricted and over the next 12 years an estimated 2.7 million people left for the West. To stop this flight, the Soviet regime built the Berlin Wall, almost overnight, in 1961. It became a symbol of the political differences between East and West, an ideological barrier known as the Iron Curtain.

In the 1980s, the communist governments across Eastern Europe began to weaken and when Hungary opened its border, many East Germans fled. Under pressure, the regime announced it would allow its citizens to travel abroad. On the same day, November 9, 1989, thousands of people flocked to the Berlin Wall, demanding to be allowed to cross. The East German guards let them pass, and people started to smash down the Wall. By October 1990, the Wall had been reduced to rubble, and Germany was reunified as one country. Communism had failed in Europe.

Scaling the Berlin Wall
East German border guards look on as Berliners climb a section of the Berlin Wall on November 10, 1989, the day after people first began tearing it down.

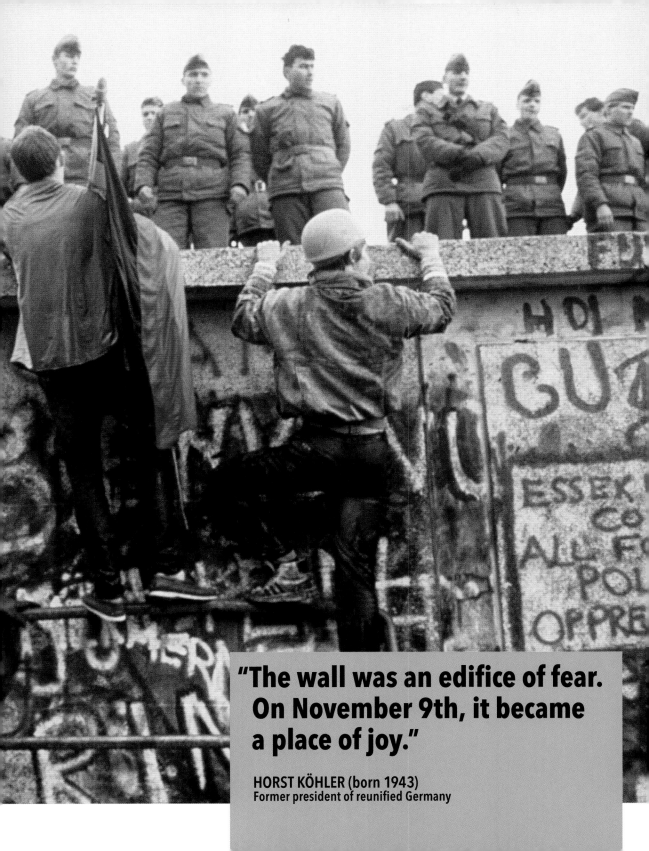

"The wall was an edifice of fear.
On November 9th, it became
a place of joy."

HORST KÖHLER (born 1943)
Former president of reunified Germany

"Neoliberalization has meant... the financialization of everything."

DAVID HARVEY (born 1935)
British-born economic geographer and anthropologist

NEOLIBERALISM is...

AN ECONOMIC AND POLITICAL POLICY THAT PROMOTES FREE TRADE, PRIVATIZATION, AND CUTS TO GOVERNMENT SPENDING

SEE ALSO:

Neoliberalism is an extreme form of capitalism. Supporters of neoliberalism argue that all economic processes—trade, industry, businesses, and financial institutions—should be free to operate and create wealth without government rules and restrictions. Since the 1970s, when governments first began to adopt neoliberal ideas, neoliberalism has had a profound impact on economies and people's lives.

FREE MARKETS

The Austrian-born British economist Friedrich Hayek was the prime mover behind neoliberalism. He opposed the type of government investment and economic planning that had become popular during and after the economic slump known as the Great Depression in the 1930s. He argued that to avoid economic downturns the market (trade in goods and services) should be unregulated. He believed government planning was inefficient and that the law of supply and demand to determine prices and availability of goods was a better way to create a healthy economy. He also argued that state control of the economy was undemocratic, because it prevented individual choice. In the 1940s and 1950s, economists who popularized neoliberalism included Austrian-born Ludwig von Mises and the American Milton Friedman, who argued that governments should control the amount of money in circulation to stablize prices—a theory known as "monetarism."

NO SOCIETY

In the 1980s, the governments run by Conservative UK Prime Minister Margaret Thatcher and Republican US President Ronald Reagan fully embraced neoliberal policies in an attempt to boost the stagnating

British and American economies. Controls on foreign currency exchange rates were lifted, enabling money to flow between countries, and companies were opened up to foreign investors. Government involvement in trade and industry was reduced and public services such as water, energy, and transportation were privatized, allowing them to be run by private companies for profit, with fewer government subsidies.

Tax cuts were also introduced, particularly for the very rich. Underpinning the economic changes was a new emphasis on individual responsibility, summed up in Thatcher's 1987 comment: "there is no such thing as society … people must look to themselves first." This marked a departure from the post-World War II consensus that the state had a responsibility for the more vulnerable groups in society.

AUSTERITY

In the 1990s, more left-leaning governments such as President Bill Clinton's Democratic Party in the US and New Labour under Tony Blair in the UK also adopted neoliberal policies. The interdependency of national economies due to globalization encouraged free trade policies, too. Banks and financial institutions boomed until, in 2008, there was a global financial crash, followed by years of global recession. To prevent economic catastrophe, governments bailed out banks, and to deal with government debt, many introduced so-called "austerity measures" to reduce government spending. This included cuts to unemployment and sickness benefits, health services, libraries, rape crisis centers, and youth centers— reducing welfare provision and social safety nets to an absolute minimum.

IMPACT

Neoliberalism remains a dominant economic practice in the world. It has generated economic growth— with bankers, financial institutions

and global corporations making huge profits— but economies have also fluctuated. Neoliberalism has heightened wealth and income inequalities between the rich and poor. According to a study by the international charity Oxfam, since 2015, the richest one percent of the world's population has owned more wealth than the rest of the planet.

"To be conservative... is to prefer the familiar to the unknown, to prefer the tried to the untried."

MICHAEL OAKESHOTT (1901–1990)
British political theorist and philosopher

CONSERVATISM is...

A POLITICAL APPROACH THAT SUPPORTS TRADITIONAL INSTITUTIONS AND VALUES PRACTICAL SOLUTIONS

SEE ALSO:

← **Capitalism**
pages 52–53

← **Liberalism**
pages 50–51

← **Neoliberalism**
pages 56–57

The clue to understanding conservatism lies in its name. Conservatives believe in keeping—or conserving—tried and tested social and political structures that have evolved over time. They reject sudden change in favor of stability and continuity.

PRACTICAL POLITICS

Sitting on the right of the political spectrum, conservatism is often described as pragmatic. That is, conservatives value practical solutions to social and economic problems rather than solutions based on abstract political theories or ideologies. Conservatives may recognize the need for change, but emphasize that this should happen gradually. Above all, they value a well ordered society in which the rule of law is clearly defined.

A RULING CLASS

In the conservative view, society is hierarchical, consisting of different rankings or social classes. Social order is based on a division between those who are best suited to rule and those who are ruled. Traditionally, conservatives place importance on conventional family structures, the monarchy (where one exists), patriotism, and religion. The role of government is often seen as paternalistic, or fatherly, providing for the needs of people as appropriate. Valuing a strong work ethic, some conservatives believe it is the individual's responsibility to better themselves, and that the individual should be given the opportunity to do so.

LIMITED GOVERNMENT

Conservatism supports capitalism and believes in private property, free trade, low taxes, and limited government interference in trade and industry. Many conservatives promote the idea of "trickle-down economics:" as wealth is created, some will trickle down to the less well off. Since the late 20th century, some conservative governments, influenced by neoliberal economics, have supported privatization of public and welfare services.

FEAR OF REVOLUTION

Like liberalism, conservatism first emerged as a political philosophy during the 18th century. It gained its distinctive commitment to social stability, order, and tradition in reaction to the upheaval of the 1789 French Revolution. In 1790, the Anglo-Irish philosopher Edmund Burke, sometimes described as the father of modern conservatism, wrote an influential pamphlet deploring the overthrow of the French monarchy and disruption of the social order. His views laid a basis for much conservative thinking. By 1834 the British Conservative Party, which originally evolved from an Irish grouping called "Tories," was formed. Today, it is one of the oldest surviving political parties. Conservatism, however, did not remain only in Britain. Over time its principles spread around the world.

MODERN CONSERVATISM

Conservatism, in its various forms, has been very influential. In the US, the Republican Party is associated with conservative values. In Britain, it has been the dominant force in politics since 1945. Historically, in Europe and South America, conservatism has been associated with Christianity, whether Catholic or Protestant. One example is that of the center-right German Christian Democratic Union (CDU) party, formerly led by German Chancellor Angela Merkel, though its members also include non-Christians.

> ## "All within the state, nothing outside the state, nothing against the state."
> BENITO MUSSOLINI (1883-1945)
> Founder of the Italian Fascist Party and former leader of Italy

FASCISM is...

A FORM OF FAR-RIGHT NATIONALISM THAT ORGANIZES SOCIETY TO CREATE A POWERFUL AUTHORITARIAN STATE

People who support fascism are known as fascists. The word is often used loosely as an insult, to criticize any person or group that is right-wing and domineering. However, fascism in practice and as political theory is far more complex and brutal.

STRENGTH THROUGH UNITY

Fascism sits on the far right of the political scale. It is highly nationalistic, placing the strength and unity of the nation state above individual liberty and freedoms. All aspects of society and the economy are regimented to create a unified and powerful nation. In practice, a fascist regime is a single-party dictatorship, led by a charismatic leader, who is presented as the one person who can resolve a country's problems. The regime is militaristic and demands total obedience, while encouraging citizens to value and identify with the nation above all else. Propaganda, stirring speeches, and carefully choreographed visual events are designed to impress and enlist the masses. Uniformed, armed militia create fear in order to subdue opposition. Fascist regimes may use democratic processes such as elections to gain power, but then abandon them once power is obtained.

RESURGENCE

Fascism emerged out of World War I (1914–1918) and was fueled by post-war economic, social, and cultural collapse. Fascist leaders came to prominence promising to rebuild their countries and restore former glories.

Italy was the first fascist state. In 1919, Benito Mussolini founded the Italian Fascist Party. At first a socialist, he later opposed communism and its ideal of social equality. Like other fascists, he saw this as a threat to the nation.

With the help of armed squads, known as Black Shirts, Mussolini gained support and terrorized opponents. He was invited to join the government and in 1922, as Italy slipped into political chaos, he and his Black Shirts marched on Rome and seized power. Taking the title Il Duce (the leader), Mussolini established a dictatorship. He worked closely with corporations to restructure the economy, promising to make Italy a great power that would reflect the glories of ancient Rome. The regime ended in 1943 when Italian partisans (resistance fighters) executed Mussolini.

During the 1930s, fascism spread across Europe. In 1939, General Francisco Franco, whose nationalist forces had defeated republicans in Spain after a brutal civil war, took power as a dictator. His fascist Falange party ruled Spain as a dictatorship until 1975. Across the border in Portugal, in 1926 a military coup established a dictatorship. The fascist government of António de Oliveira Salazar that ensued ruled until 1974, making it Europe's most enduring fascist regime.

NATIONAL SOCIALISM

In Germany, fascism was known as National Socialism, or Nazism. Its leader, Adolf Hitler, tapped into and exploited the humiliation felt by Germany after its defeat in 1918, promising to rebuild Germany as a great military empire. Nazism dominated Germany from 1933 to 1945. Like other fascist regimes, Nazism was nationalistic and totalitarian but, unlike Italy, anti-Semitism was fundamental to its ideology (political beliefs). Placing emphasis on the idea of a pure Aryan "master race," Nazis scapegoated and sought to exterminate Jews, Roma, and other ethnic or vulnerable communities. Storm troopers and the Gestapo, the dreaded secret police, imposed military rule and quashed dissent.

NEO-FASCISM

No country or political group today would describe itself as fascist. However, the terms "neo-fascist" or "neo-Nazi" are used to describe groups or individuals who subscribe to fascist or Nazi values. In recent years, these groups have included the English Defence League in the UK and the National Rally in France. Both are strongly nationalistic and anti-immigrant. Another term that appears in the news today is "alt-right." This refers to a far-right, white supremacist movement that began in the US during the 2010s. Alt-right groups often display the Nazi swastika, are anti-Semitic, and argue for tight controls on immigrants. An active "antifa" network has emerged to oppose them.

"Never forget that everything Hitler did in Germany was 'legal'."

MARTIN LUTHER KING, JR. (1929–1968)
American minister and civil-rights activist

HITLER'S RISE TO POWER

SEPTEMBER 1919–AUGUST 1934

Following Germany's defeat in World War I (1914–1918), ex-German Army corporal Adolf Hitler saw an opportunity to stir up support for his far-right National Socialist (Nazi) Party. He convinced people that the Nazis could make a humiliated Germany great again.

Hitler joined the nationalist German Workers' Party (later the Nazi Party) in 1919 and, with a talent for public speaking, became the party's leader in 1921. But popular support was slow to come, and when Hitler led the party in a failed attempt to overthrow the German government in 1923, he was imprisoned for treason.

National reports of his trial made Hitler a public figure. On his release, he pursued power using propaganda and intimidation. Blaming "outsiders" such as communists and Jewish people for the political and economic chaos of Germany, he united the nation against these so-called enemies, and support for the Nazis grew. In 1933, with his party not yet in power, Hitler became Chancellor (head of government) through a backstairs political deal.

A few weeks later, an unexplained fire broke out in the *Reichstag* (parliament). Blaming communists, Hitler pushed through an Enabling Act allowing him to pass laws without parliament's consent. He used it to ban all opposition. In 1934, Hitler seized absolute power and declared himself *Führer* (Leader). His tyrannical fascist dictatorship would lead the world to war again in 1939.

Power and glory

Hitler climbs the steps at the 1934 Bückeberg Harvest Festival. The Nazis used the powerful appeal of uniforms, symbols, and salutes to rally popular support.

> "I am not an individual–I am the people."
> HUGO CHÁVEZ (1954–2013)
> Former president of Venezuela

POPULISM is...

A POLITICAL STRATEGY THAT CLAIMS TO SPEAK UP FOR THE CONCERNS OF ORDINARY PEOPLE AGAINST A PRIVILEGED OR CORRUPT ELITE

The term "populism" has appeared frequently in the media over the last decade. Associated with politicians such as Donald Trump (US), Marine Le Pen (France), and the Podemos party in Spain, populism is on the rise. A political approach used by both right- and left-wing political parties or movements, populism promotes the idea that society is divided into two groups—"the people" and the "elite"—that are pitted against each other.

CHARISMATIC LEADERS

Populist leaders are often described as "demagogues," charismatic, larger-than-life individuals who are skilled in whipping up a crowd. They may be identified with a political party or not, but present themselves as advocates of the people. In the populist view, "the people" are portrayed as pure individuals, morally superior to the "elite," which is seen as corrupt, anti-democratic, and self-interested.

EMOTIVE LANGUAGE

Strategically, a populist leader uses emotive language to tap into the deep-seated anxieties of their supporters, who feel betrayed by those in power. During his campaign to become US president in 2016, Donald Trump constantly referred to "draining the swamp," by which he meant he would rid the US government of what he alleged was its corruption. Voicing concern for democracy is another recurring feature. During the 2010s, Nigel Farage, as leader of the United Kingdom Independence Party (UKIP), gained support for his populist anti-European Union (EU) campaign by claiming that the EU was undemocratic and calling for the return of British sovereignty. In this way, populist politicians may use democratic channels to gain influence, but seek to undermine these systems of government once they are in power.

POPULIST MOVEMENTS

The 2008 financial crisis, economic hardship, and social inequality have encouraged support for a number of short-lived, broadly left-wing populist movements. These have included the international Occupy movement, which highlighted economic and social injustice with the slogan "We are the 99%" and the Spanish anti-austerity, left-wing political party, Podemos. The populist *gilets jaunes* (yellow vests) also took to the streets in 2018 to protest against the French government.

TAKING POWER

Opposition to ethnic minorities and the movement of refugees of war have helped to trigger support for populism. So too has the perception that not all groups in society have benefitted from globalization. Populist political parties have played on such issues to enter government. On the left, populist leaders and parties have included the late Venezuelan president Hugo Chávez, whose party was in

power until his death in 2013. The Greek party Syriza, a coalition of left-wing radicals that formed a government in 2015, attributed Greece's economic woes to the policies of traditional political parties. Many modern populist parties and leaders are right wing. Some take a nationalist and an anti-immigrant stance. They attack what they see as an intellectual and liberal elite that permits access for migrants. They include Marine Le Pen's National Rally in France and Viktor Orbán, Prime Minster of Hungary. Although these leaders present themselves as true democrats, in practice they resent democratic debate, seeking to take control of and limit freedom of the press.

APPEAL

The appeal of populism is that it speaks directly to the people, overcoming the "elites," and it appears to offer simple solutions to complex situations. Its rise reflects a distancing of the electorate from traditional political parties, which are viewed as removed from the lives of ordinary people. Populist ideas spread rapidly through social media, but their apparent simplicity can encourage the spread of misinformation.

"From this day forward, a new vision will govern our land... America first."

DONALD TRUMP (born 1946)
US President, speaking at his inauguration in 2016

THE ELECTION OF DONALD TRUMP

November 8, 2016

In 2016, Donald Trump of the Republican Party was elected 45th president of the US in a surprise victory. A maverick political outsider, Trump used a populist strategy to appeal to the electorate.

Donald Trump's support came from voters who had felt neglected by successive past politicians and wanted radical change. Trump, a brash reality-TV personality who refused to stick to the script, tapped into this discontent.

A beneficiary of his father's real-estate empire, Trump had never held an elected political office. He presented himself as "anti-establishment"—opposed to the groups in society that consistently held the most power. His populist language set the "people" against the "elite" as he vowed to give power to the people, stirring up crowds with chants to lock up his rival for president, Hillary Clinton of the Democratic Party. Trump used Twitter to communicate with his supporters, bypassing traditional news media, which he attacked as "fake news."

Trump's crowd-pleasing promises included tax cuts, putting "America first" in trade deals and foreign policy, denying climate change, and dismissing clean energy in favor of jobs in coal mining. When presented with complex problems, such as immigration, he offered simple solutions, like building a wall along the US–Mexico border to keep immigrants out. Trump won the election, taking 304 electoral college votes, to Clinton's 227, though Clinton gained 48.5 percent of the popular vote to Trump's 46.4 percent.

Trump vows to "Make America Great Again"
With a day to go before the election, Trump addresses a campaign rally in North Carolina, appealing to people in states that felt left behind by globalization.

State and
SOCIETY

A CONSTITUTION is...

Birth of the US Constitution

HUMAN RIGHTS are...

Montgomery bus boycott

SEPARATION OF POWERS is...

POLITICAL DEBATE is...

An ELECTION is...

Elections in India

SUFFRAGE is...

Mary Wollstonecraft

FEDERALISM is...

A COUP D'ÉTAT is...

HOW DOES DEMOCRACY WORK?

ARE ALL PEOPLE IN THE WORLD ENTITLED TO BASIC HUMAN RIGHTS?

CAN EVERYONE **VOTE** IN AN **ELECTION**, REGARDLESS OF **RACE** OR **GENDER**?

ARE **CIVIL RIGHTS** THE SAME AS HUMAN RIGHTS?

SHOULD **VOTING BE COMPULSORY** FOR ALL **ADULTS**?

WHAT **FREEDOMS** AND **RESPONSIBILITIES** ARE SET OUT IN A **CONSTITUTION?**

HOW DO DIFFERENT **ELECTORAL SYSTEMS** AFFECT THE OUTCOME OF ELECTIONS?

Democracy is a system of government that gives people the power to choose who they want to govern them. To make sure a state is fair and free, it needs the consent of society.

Democratic states are built on a belief in human and civil rights. These may be enshrined in a constitution, which is an agreement that sets out the relationship between the government and the people in society.

The government in a democracy is elected by the people, who vote for representatives to make decisions about how to govern the country on their behalf.

The institutions of government in charge of running the state vary from country to country, but generally include a congress, parliament, or assembly, a president or prime minister, and a legal system. These work together to make decisions and keep each other in check.

WHAT IS THE ROLE OF AN ELECTED CONGRESS OR ASSEMBLY?

WHAT'S THE DIFFERENCE BETWEEN A PRESIDENT AND A PRIME MINISTER?

WHAT DOES THE GOVERNMENT ACTUALLY DO?

WHAT ARE EMERGENCY POWERS?

WHAT DOES THE LEGAL SYSTEM HAVE TO DO WITH RUNNING A COUNTRY?

WHO DECIDES WHAT IN A FEDERAL, STATE, OR DEVOLVED GOVERNMENT?

> ## "Law is the expression of the general will... It must be the same for all, whether it protects or punishes."
>
> **DECLARATION OF THE RIGHTS OF MAN AND OF THE CITIZEN (1789)**
> Issued by the National Assembly of France

A CONSTITUTION is...

A SET OF RULES ABOUT HOW A COUNTRY IS GOVERNED AND WHAT LEGAL RIGHTS ITS CITIZENS HAVE

SEE ALSO:

← **The French Revolution** pages 18–19

→ **Birth of the US Constitution** pages 74–75

→ **Separation of powers** pages 80–81

Written or unwritten, a constitution is a set of rules about how a country should be governed, how power is shared, and what rights and protections its citizens possess under the law.

In most countries, these rules are set out in a single document. The first US Constitution, drafted in 1787, had 4,400 words and was four pages long, and India's constitution, adopted in 1949, ran to 145,000 words over 232 pages. In contrast to these single documents, the UK's constitution is formed of Acts of Parliament, court judgments, and political customs established over hundreds of years.

VALUES AND ASPIRATIONS

More than just a set of rules, a constitution is an expression of a country's political identity.

It often begins with a short statement (known as a preamble) that briefly summarizes what that country stands for by setting out the ideals it wishes to embrace.

For example, India highlights justice, liberty, equality, and fraternity in its preamble, whereas Ireland states that it wishes to "promote the common good, with due observance of Prudence, Justice, and Charity." Although these two statements use different terminology, both are intended to inspire their citizens—and their elected representatives—and encourage them to be ambitious in their efforts to measure up to their country's chosen ideals.

RIGHTS OF CITIZENS

A central part of any constitution is the rights of citizens. In 1776, the American colonies' Declaration of Independence set out the basic rights of their citizens to "Life, Liberty, and the pursuit of Happiness." Just a few years later, in 1789, the Declaration of the Rights of Man and of the Citizen proclaimed in revolutionary France that "Men are born and remain free and equal in rights."

These two historic declarations, which set out the founding principles of the new republics of the United States and France, had a major impact, influencing the constitutions and human rights charters of democracies around the world today.

WHERE POWER LIES

A constitution normally sets out what powers are held by the state's three branches of government: the executive (the government of the day, led by a president or prime minister), the legislature (the lawmaking assembly), and the judiciary (the law courts). It also provides details about how a president or prime minister is accountable (answerable) to the branches of government and how he or she may be chosen—and, if necessary, removed.

Within this system of power-sharing, the constitution identifies where sovereignty lies. In the US, the ultimate political authority rests with the people and this is acknowledged in the preamble to the constitution, which begins, "We the People...." In the UK, sovereignty lies with the Crown-in-Parliament, but the queen (or king) defers to the prime minister and has a largely ceremonial role, while parliament, representing the people, is the highest legislative authority.

To ensure fair and effective representation of the people, a constitution may set out rules for elections, such as who is entitled to take part; when and how elections are held; how the results are decided; and who is responsible for enforcing these rules.

SET IN STONE?

In most democracies, a constitution is seen as a "living" document, which it should be possible to adapt or change. Accordingly, it must set out how it may be amended, so that it can continue to reflect the values and principles of the time and embrace issues that may not have been seen as important or relevant when the constitution was first written.

However, a constitution sits above all other laws, and no single person or group has the power to alter it. It can only be changed through the widest possible consensus—by a majority vote of elected representatives or in a public referendum.

BIRTH OF THE US CONSTITUTION

1776–1791

The political structures of many nations have evolved over time, but the American Republic came into existence with a purpose-built constitution. This defined a framework for government, while limiting its power, and gave American citizens legal rights.

In 1776, the 13 colonies along the eastern coast of America resolved to shake off British rule. On July 4, these fledgling states declared their independence and went on to defeat Britain in the American Revolution in 1783.

At a Constitutional Convention held in Philadelphia in 1787, 55 delegates debated how to govern their new Republic. They wrote a formal Constitution, which came into effect in 1789 and was amended with the Bill of Rights in 1791. The document laid out a system of government with checks and balances between Congress, the President, and the courts to curb excessive power. It also addressed the tensions between a federal (national) government and the fiercely independent states.

The United States of America now has 50 states, but the Constitution still shapes the country today. Political debate often cites its principles, such as the rights to free speech and assembly enshrined in the First Amendment, and the Second Amendment right to bear arms. With 27 amendments between 1791 and 1992, the US Constitution continues to evolve and to define its nation.

Signing of the US Constitution in 1787
This painting shows the 39 delegates who signed the US Constitution. George Washington, who became the first US president, presides over the Convention.

"I am persuaded no constitution was ever before so well calculated as ours."

THOMAS JEFFERSON (1743–1826)
Founding Father and third president of the US

> # "To deny people their human rights is to challenge their very humanity."
> **NELSON MANDELA (1918–2013)**
> Civil-rights activist and former president of South Africa

HUMAN RIGHTS are...

STANDARDS AND LAWS THAT ALLOW ALL PEOPLE TO LIVE WITH DIGNITY, FREEDOM, EQUALITY, JUSTICE, AND PEACE

Human rights are fundamental ways of living and being treated that every human on the planet deserves, by virtue of being human. A government that does not respect its citizens' rights risks losing their support and therefore its right to rule.

A LONG HISTORY
Persia's Cyrus the Great published laws protecting the rights of his subjects in 539 BCE, but neither he nor the rest of the ancient world saw such rights as belonging equally to all. It was England's Magna Carta of 1215 that first established the principle of equality before the law. In 1689, English philosopher John Locke presented the idea of "natural rights" as an essential part of being human, and defined them as the rights to "life, liberty, and property."

The US Declaration of Independence in 1776 proclaimed that "all men are created equal" and endowed with certain "inalienable" rights of which no one should be deprived. The French Revolution of 1789 declared that "Men are born and remain free and equal in rights… These rights are liberty, property, safety, and resistance against oppression."

After World War II, the United Nations (UN) adopted the Universal Declaration of Human Rights in 1948. This set out 30 basic human rights that included the right to free speech, a fair trial, and protection from torture, as well as economic, social, and cultural rights such as adequate food, decent housing, education, health, access to clean water, and work.

Societies have long debated the relative importance of freedom from state interference as opposed to the right to have certain needs met.

CIVIL RIGHTS
While human rights are—in theory, at least—fundamental rights that are universal the world over, civil

rights refer to the laws and customs that protect an individual's freedom in a given country, and vary from country to country. Activists for civil rights the world over demand equal opportunities and protection under the law, regardless of race, religion, and economic status.

The US civil rights movement, for example, sought to secure full political, social, and economic rights for African Americans in the post-war period from 1946 to 1968. A series of Civil Rights Acts outlawed racism and discrimination, the last one just weeks after the assassination of civil rights leader Martin Luther King, Jr. in 1968.

However, the civil rights gains of the past half-century have stalled in the US, despite the election of the nation's first African American president, Barack Obama, in 2008. The unjust killing of a black teenager in Florida in 2012 sparked the Black Lives Matter movement, which demands equal treatment for African Americans by the criminal justice system.

Other groups have asserted their civil rights, too. Since the 1960s, women, people with disabilities, the LGBTQ community, and other groups have pushed for their inclusion in society and equal rights, in activist movements around the world.

MORE TO BE DONE

The UN continues to draft new laws and invest vast sums in protecting and promoting human (and civil) rights worldwide. For example, the 1979 UN convention outlawing discrimination against women has inspired women's rights groups in patriarchal societies. However, while most countries support the UN in the fight against the sexual exploitation and abuse of women and children, there is no quick fix and the abuse continues.

Campaign groups such as Human Rights Watch and Amnesty International pressure governments to address human rights issues. So do economic and political sanctions imposed by other countries, but at the risk of provoking a backlash and adding to people's suffering.

On a smaller scale, sports organizations can boycott competitions in countries where human rights are routinely abused. At a personal level, consumers can make ethical choices about where they shop and go on vacation, for example, to avoid financially propping up abusive regimes.

"Our mistreatment was just not right, and I was tired of it."

ROSA PARKS (1913–2005)
American civil-rights activist

MONTGOMERY BUS BOYCOTT
DECEMBER 1955–DECEMBER 1956

When one woman refused to give up her bus seat in Montgomery, Alabama, her individual action led to the first mass protest against racial segregation in the US, paving the way for the American civil rights movement.

On December 1, 1955, 42-year-old Rosa Parks took the bus home from her job as a seamstress. At the time, racist laws segregated black and white people on public transportation. As the bus filled up, the driver asked Parks and three other black passengers to give up their seats in the first row of the "colored" section to white people. Parks refused, and was arrested.

News of Parks' arrest spread rapidly through Montgomery's black community and its leaders, including a young church minister named Martin Luther King, Jr., who decided to start a boycott of the bus system. From December 5, 1955, the day Parks stood trial, around 40,000 African Americans—75 percent of the city's bus users— refused to travel on the bus, instead walking, taking cabs, or sharing cars. The boycott lasted 381 days, attracting national attention. Its impact on the local economy was huge.

On December, 20, 1956, the Supreme Court ruled that racial segregation on public transportation was unconstitutional. The boycott ended the next day. Montgomery was a powerful message for both black and white people that results could be achieved by nonviolent means. The event helped shape the American civil rights movement and inspired the campaigns of its future leader, Martin Luther King, Jr.

Civil rights success
Marking the end of the Montgomery Bus Boycott, Rosa Parks boards a Montgomery bus in December 1956. Her actions had led to the end of racial segregation on buses.

> "Power ought to serve as a check to power."
> BARON DE MONTESQUIEU (1689-1755)
> French philosopher

SEPARATION OF POWERS is...

A MODEL OF GOVERNMENT THAT SHARES RESPONSIBILITY AMONG THREE DISTINCT GROUPS SO THAT NONE HAS TOO MUCH POWER

In a modern democracy, each of the three core functions of government—making laws, putting them into practice, and interpreting the law—is held by a separate branch of government.

THE THREE BRANCHES

The branch of government that makes and amends laws is known as the legislature. This takes the form of a parliament or assembly (or Congress in the US), which is usually made up of representatives elected by the public. They belong to different groups, known as political parties, and together they propose, examine, and debate policies—ideas for how to improve citizens' lives and make society work, which may require new laws—and vote to approve or reject them.

The president or prime minister is head of the executive. This is the branch responsible for running a country by implementing the policies and laws passed by the legislature. The executive is made up of a small group called the cabinet, appointed by the president or prime minister, and is often referred to as the government. The executive works with an unelected bureaucracy, the civil service, to put policies and laws into practice.

The legal system of a country is its judiciary, the branch of government that interprets laws and delivers judgments through the courts. It is made up of judges and other legal experts, who are appointed to see that the law is applied to everyone, including the other two branches. The idea of the separation of powers was first introduced in ancient Greece, the birthplace of democracy, and in the Roman Republic. But it was the 18th-century French judge and political philosopher Montesquieu who developed it into today's tripartite (three-part) model.

This separation is designed to prevent one branch from becoming too powerful by making it accountable (answerable) to the others. Each branch of government has some control over the actions of the other two branches and may amend or veto (block) their actions.

PRESIDENT OR PARLIAMENT

The separation of powers is at its clearest in a presidential democracy, such as the US. Usually the president (the executive leader) is elected by the people and is independent, not answerable to the legislature.

In a parliamentary system, the executive (the people who form a government) is taken from the legislature (parliament) and remains accountable to it. The political party that receives the majority of the public's votes forms the new government

and elects a leader, the prime minister. In this system, the prime minister is head of government, while the head of state is usually a ceremonial president (or a constitutional monarch), who is a non-political focus of national identity. Some countries, including Germany, France, and India, have both a president and a prime minister who share the responsibilities of leadership in a semi-presidential system.

HOLDING POWER TO ACCOUNT

When the public votes for a government, it is voting for a certain political party or candidate's promises of how they will govern the country. These promises, which are set out during an election and later become policies, explain how the government plans to do such things as fund schools or tackle climate change.

In order for the public to know whether the government it has put into power is acting in its interests and sticking to these promises, the system of checks and balances enables it to be held to account by the other two branches of government. This requirement for a government to explain its actions or its failure to act is at the heart of any fully functioning democracy.

EXECUTIVE

LEGISLATURE

JUDICIARY

"Dialogue is the essence of
parliamentary politics."
SHARAD PAWAR (born 1940)
Prominent Indian politician

POLITICAL DEBATE is ...

THE PROCESS BY WHICH POLITICIANS IN A PARLIAMENTARY DEMOCRACY MAKE DECISIONS ABOUT HOW TO RUN A COUNTRY

SEE ALSO:

← **Democracy**
pages 32-33

← **Separation of powers**
pages 80-81

→ **An election**
pages 84-85

D ebate—formal discussion of an issue in a public meeting place—is at the heart of parliamentary democracy. The word "parliament" comes from the French verb *parler*, meaning to talk, and in a democracy people elect representatives to do exactly

that. Debate is how a parliament— or a national assembly, or Congress in the US—fulfills its role of representing the people, checking what the government is doing (including taxing and spending), and making or changing laws.

POLITICAL PARTIES
Central to the democratic process of debate are the modern political parties—organized groups of people who share similar ideas about how their country should be governed. They may stand for an

ideology (such as conservatism, liberalism, or socialism) or a particular issue (such as the environment). Political parties exist in most countries around the world, unless blocked by dictatorships. Countries may have a one-party, two-party, or a multiparty system. A one-party state, such as China or North Korea, does not give citizens a choice of parties and policies to vote for in an election, and is undemocratic.

SHAPING GOVERNMENT POLICY

Before an election, each party decides its policies—a course of action on matters such as education, crime, or the economy—and issues a manifesto of pledges to voters. The party (or coalition of parties) that wins the election agrees an annual agenda of what it will ask the parliament to discuss, and a "speaker" is chosen to chair the debates.

The pledges parties make, and the criticisms they make about rival parties—both during an election and in parliament, in press interviews, and on social media —all form part of the wider political debate. Many people find the adversarial style of party politics off-putting, and distrust politicians who exaggerate their achievements and insult one another. Some people doubt this debate helps society, and never vote. However, parties provide a collective voice in parliament, and a valuable link between state and society.

Groups working in the interests of citizens, such as charities and trade unions, as well as businesses and individuals lobby (or try to influence) parties and government to take on board their concerns. Activists, too, try to apply pressure, by organizing protests online and in the streets to demand change.

Wherever these forms of debate take place—in national and local government, in the media, or in the streets—freedom of speech is essential to ensuring that people's views are heard.

HOLDING GOVERNMENT TO ACCOUNT

In a democracy, it is the role of the opposition—the parties not in power—to hold to account the party (or coalition of parties) that is in power. They do this in parliament by questioning the government about its actions or failure to act on promises it has made to the electorate.

If a government in a parliamentary democracy is failing to manage the country and a national crisis occurs, the parliament may debate a "vote of no confidence" in the government. This can trigger an election to replace the government. In the US and other presidential countries, if a president is accused of abusing their position of power, Congress or the national assembly debates whether they should be "impeached"—charges made against them that are serious enough to result in their removal from office.

> "The English think they are free.
> They are free only during the
> election of members of parliament."
>
> JEAN-JACQUES ROUSSEAU (1712–1778)
> Genevan philosopher

AN ELECTION is...

A PROCESS IN WHICH PEOPLE VOTE TO CHOOSE A PERSON TO HOLD AN OFFICIAL POSITION IN AN ASSEMBLY OR OTHER FORM OF GOVERNMENT

In a representative democracy, people vote for politicians who stand in an election to represent them in an assembly or parliament. In some countries, voters elect a president, too. Elections are held in many other walks of life, from student councils in schools to trade unions at work, to give people a voice in deciding how things are done, but the elections that choose a new government affect all of us.

In these elections, voters choose a candidate based on the political party they represent and how closely the party's policies are line up with the voters' views and beliefs. Each party publishes its policies in a platform or manifesto—a set of promises the party wants to put into action if it is elected to govern the country. But voters may also be swayed by the candidate's personality and reputation.

FIRST PAST THE POST

Different countries use different electoral systems to elect assembly members, congressmen and women, or members of parliament (MPs) in the UK, and each system produces a different kind of result.

In "first past the post" (FPTP), also known as a majoritarian system, the candidate who wins the majority of votes in a constituency (or local voting district) is elected as an MP. In a parliamentary democracy, the party that has the most candidates elected forms the new government.

This system, or variations of it, is used in around one third of the world's countries, including the UK, the US, Canada, France, and India. It favors large parties, which are often long established and well known to voters. But it can work against newer, smaller parties with particular interests, such as the environment.

Candidates of a minority group rarely attract a majority of votes, so their interests may be neglected in congress or parliament.

PARTY LIST

Many countries favor electoral systems based on proportional representation (PR). With some variation, these count the number of votes cast for a party across the whole country rather than in each district. In the form known as Party List PR, voters gain representatives roughly in proportion to the total number of votes cast for their party. This gives smaller parties a better chance of winning seats than under the majoritarian system.

This may seem fairer, but it often means there is no outright majority for one party, so two or more parties go into partnership, or coalition. Coalition governments may find it hard to agree on policy and can be unable to get things done, and so may not last long. Italy, which until 1994 used the Party List system, had 65 governments in the 70 years after World War II.

MIXED SYSTEMS

Along with political instability, another disadvantage of PR is that voters do not know their elected representatives. For this reason, some countries use systems that combine proportional representation of parties with the election of local candidates. The Additional Member System, used in Germany, New Zealand, and by the UK's Welsh and Scottish assemblies, is one such system.

Northern Ireland, though part of the UK, also has its own assembly, which is elected by a system known as the Single Transferable Vote. This allows voters to rank candidates in order of preference in order to elect a power-sharing executive—a coalition of rival parties, set up as part of the peace process after the violent sectarian conflict of 1969–1998.

A REFERENDUM

In direct democracy, the people rather than their representatives decide an issue—often in a referendum, when the government hands the responsibility for making a decision on a particular topic to the public.

In 2016 in the UK, for example, the population voted on whether to leave or remain in the European Union. Switzerland has been holding referendums since 1798 and has held more than any other country. Between 1996 and 2016 alone, it had 180 referendums, on issues ranging from introducing car-free Sundays to rejecting plans to abolish the army.

"True democracy cannot be worked by 20 men sitting at the center. It has to be worked from below, by each village."

MAHATMA GANDHI (1869–1948)
Civil-rights activist and leader of India's independence movement

ELECTIONS IN INDIA

APRIL–MAY 2019

With a population of 1.3 billion, India is the world's biggest democracy: around 900 million citizens—men and women aged 18 and above—are eligible to vote.

India is a federal republic with a parliamentary democracy. Its elections are a big undertaking. In a country covering 1.269 million sq miles (3.287 million sq km), parts of rural India are very remote, yet polling stations travel within 1.2 miles (2 km) of every voter. Elections take place over six weeks, and votes are cast on electronic machines that display the symbols of the candidates' political parties. One quarter of Indians are illiterate, so they recognize party logos rather than names. Officials bring the machines over the Himalayas on foot, through forests by elephant, and across deserts by camel.

India has a Hindu majority, but more than 300 million Indians belong to religious minorities, including 200 million Muslims. With Hindu nationalism on the rise in the 21st century, recent elections have been marred by violence and voter suppression, notably of Muslims and the Dalits (who form the lowest caste, or hereditary class, in Hindu society).

India's 2014 election was nicknamed the "social media election" with the big parties now spending millions on wooing voters via targeted messages. This unregulated digital campaigning is a global trend that challenges strict codes of campaign conduct that help to ensure free and fair elections.

Waiting to vote

These women in Northern India show their voter registration papers while waiting to cast their ballot in the 2019 general election. Of the 8,000 candidates running for 543 parliamentary seats, only 8.8 percent were women.

> ## "Voting is the most precious right of every citizen."
> ### HILLARY RODHAM CLINTON (born 1947)
> Former US Secretary of State

SUFFRAGE is...

THE RIGHT FOR PEOPLE TO VOTE IN A POLITICAL ELECTION–IDEALLY REGARDLESS OF RACE, GENDER, WEALTH, OR SOCIAL STATUS

The right to vote is fundamental to modern democracy, but the history of suffrage is long and complex. In ancient Greece, only adult male citizens could vote; women and slaves were not citizens and had no vote. Even after the American and French revolutions of the 1700s, inspired by ideals of liberty and equality, only property-owning white men could vote.

In the 1800s, campaigners for workers' rights and suffragists, who supported votes for women, fought to extend voting rights. In the US, this struggle was linked to anti-slavery groups and the right to vote for black people, while in the UK, suffragettes took violent action for women's right to vote. New Zealand was the first country to give women the vote, in 1893.

A generation later, World War I ended the age of empire and the old hierarchies. In 1918, most women over the age of 30 in the UK gained the vote, and all men over the age of 21; that was extended in 1928 to include all women over the age of 21, lowered to 18 in 1969.

Similarly in the US, women first became eligible to vote in 1920, and the minimum voting age was lowered to 18 in 1971. But it was not until 2015 that women in Saudi Arabia gained suffrage.

UNIVERSAL SUFFRAGE

The ongoing battle for universal suffrage—when every adult citizen has the right to vote, regardless of gender, ethnicity, or income—has proved long and hard.

In many countries, people of color didn't win suffrage until decades after white women. In Australia, it took until 1962 for the country's indigenous (Aboriginal) people to win the right to vote in all states. In the US, the 1965 Voting Rights Act finally outlawed making voters pass literacy tests, which had mostly discriminated against African Americans. South Africa held its first election with universal suffrage in 1994, after decades of apartheid (a system of racial segregation) restricting voting rights.

VOTER SUPPRESSION

While suffrage (also known as political franchise) is widely recognized as a fundamental human right, it is not yet fully enforced for millions of individuals around the world. Consistently disenfranchised groups include noncitizens (any individual who is not a national of the state in which they live), those who commit crimes, the homeless, the poor, and those who fear reprisal from voting. In patriarchal societies, women are told how to vote, or prevented from voting at all. In Afghanistan, under strict Islamic codes, a woman needs permission from a male guardian to leave the home, making it difficult to vote.

To combat disenfranchisement, local and international monitoring groups assist governments to hold free and fair elections by observing the whole process—from voter education and candidates' campaigns to arrangements for where people cast their vote and how the final vote is counted.

ENCOURAGING PARTICIPATION

Many people have the right to vote freely, but choose not to. In an effort to engage more people to take part in the electoral process, about a dozen countries have lowered the minimum voting age to 16—including Argentina, Brazil, Ecuador, and Austria.

In some countries, voting is mandatory. In Australia, for example, failing to vote can result in a fine. Some suggest voting should be made compulsory only for young people eligible to vote for the first time. Once people vote, they are much more likely to continue voting throughout their lives. Such a move would not only increase the participation of young people in democracy, but could ensure that political parties paid more attention to their concerns.

Mary Wollstonecraft

1759–1797

Anglo-Irish radical writer and philosopher Mary Wollstonecraft was not called a "feminist" in her own time; the term would not be used for nearly another 100 years. She was, however, one of the earliest champions of women's equality and she argued that girls should receive the same education as boys. Her advanced ideas laid an early foundation stone for the women's rights movements of later centuries.

> "Strengthen the female mind by enlarging it and there will be the end of blind obedience."

The rights of women

In the 1700s, it was unthinkable for women to have the vote or a professional career. Wollstonecraft believed that, given equal opportunities with men, women could be set free from domestic slavery. In 1792, she published the book that made her famous: *A Vindication of the Rights of Women*, one of the earliest feminist texts. In it, she argued for women to be educated as more than "alluring mistresses" of men, learning rather to "unfold their faculties," dignified by the ability and right to support themselves.

Life cut short

That year, fired up by the ideals of the French Revolution, she went to Paris. There, she had an affair with a man by whom she had a daughter, Fanny. By 1795, Wollstonecraft was back in London. She had a happy marriage to writer William Godwin in 1797 but, sharing the fate of many 18th-century women, she died after giving birth, at the age of 38. Her work, rediscovered by women's rights activists a century later, still resonates with feminists today.

Famous daughter
Wollstonecraft's second daughter, whose birth she did not survive, became famous as Mary Shelley, author of the Gothic novel *Frankenstein* (1818). Like her mother, Shelley, was aware of the injustices faced by women.

"A hyena in petticoats"
This is what writer Horace Walpole (1717–1797) called Mary Wollstonecraft, in a typical male reaction of the time. John Opie's 1791 portrait was seen as unconventional. Women were not usually painted looking boldly at the viewer.

Self-taught

The childhood of London-born Mary Wollstonecraft was blighted by a bullying, alcoholic father. Like many girls of the time, she received little formal schooling. She managed to educate herself enough to fill some of the gaps in her knowledge and by her early twenties had opened a small school. When the venture failed, she fell back on the little work then available for middle-class women, such as live-in jobs as a companion or a children's tutor. By now, Wollstonecraft was shaping her ideas on the lack of freedom and education for women. She began to move in intellectual circles, befriending radical thinkers of the day.

> ## "The powers delegated... to the federal government are few and defined."
> **JAMES MADISON (1751-1836)**
> Founding Father and fourth president of the US

FEDERALISM is...

A WAY OF DISTRIBUTING POWER BETWEEN CENTRAL AND REGIONAL GOVERNMENT

In a federal system of government, a group of regions or states agrees to unite under, and share power with, a central authority, which forms a federal (national) government. They decide which aspects of political power the regions will retain, and which they will hand over to the center, so that regional and federal governments have separate tasks that they are responsible for carrying out.

FEDERALISM IN THE US

Federalism is often found in large nations—such as the US, Canada, Brazil, Germany, India, Russia, and Australia—each made up of once separate colonies or states.

It was the US that set up the world's first modern federal government, in 1787. Congress (the US federal assembly) divides its power among the country's 50 states (for example, California, New York, and Texas). These states have a considerable amount of autonomy, or control over how they govern, which they have negotiated with Congress in order to preserve their individual liberties, interests, and diversity.

Setting up local schools is one example of an area of policy over which individual US states have ultimate control. Another is law and order: some states allow the death penalty for serious offenses, other states do not. Some policies are coordinated with the federal government, including taxation, business regulation, civil rights, and the environment, while the federal government has ultimate control over key areas such as the army, foreign policy and declaring war, international trade deals, the postal service, and issuing money.

WHO'S IN CHARGE?

Under the US Constitution, which sets out the overarching laws that govern the country, Congress is the highest legislative power in the

UNITARY STATES

In a unitary state (one governed as a single power, not a federation), the central national government holds all the political authority, and regional government operates under its control. Laws are created by the central government and apply to the entire nation and its citizens.

One example of a unitary state is the UK, formed of four countries: England, Scotland, Wales, and Northern Ireland. Its central government devolves (transfers) authority to the regions to enable them to carry out certain tasks, but it still maintains direct control over them and can decide to take back those powers.

land. Individual states are required by law to conform with federal decisions—if a state proposes something that contradicts federal law, Congress can overrule it. But a state can also block federal legislation by refusing to ratify it. This system allows states a good deal of freedom to make their own political decisions, but it may also cause conflict between federal and state governments. In the US and elsewhere, negotiation between the center and the regions is a key aspect of federalism, helping national and regional government to coexist.

The same is true of a confederation—a group of nations that come together to agree on issues that affect them all. After World War II, for example, what is now called the European Union (EU) was set up to negotiate peaceful economic and political cooperation between its member nations. The EU has some federal institutions, such as a parliament and a Court of Justice, but it is not a unified federal "superstate"—EU members retain the power to amend its treaties.

LOCAL POLITICS

Whatever the division of power between a national government and the regions of a country, much of daily life is run at a more local level, in cities, towns, and rural districts. Local politicians and councils are elected by residents to oversee day-to-day needs, such as garbage collection, water supply, and emergency services. Some issues, such as urban planning and transportation, may be coordinated across local, regional, and national government.

This multi-level process gives people more control over decisions that affect their lives. Local politicians also serve in regional and national assemblies, where local needs may prompt bigger decisions that help the nation as a whole.

> "To put on the garment of legitimacy
> is the first aim of every coup."
> BARBARA W. TUCHMAN (1912–1989)
> American historian and writer

A COUP D'ÉTAT is...

THE FORCIBLE OVERTHROW OF A GOVERNMENT BY A SMALL GROUP OF PEOPLE WHO HOLD POLITICAL OR MILITARY AUTHORITY

Unlike a coup's power grab from above, a revolution is a mass uprising of the people that seeks to bring about sweeping changes to the way a country is organized, from top to bottom.

A "coup d'état" is a French term, meaning literally a blow against the state. It refers to a government being overthrown—illegally and often violently—by an opposing political or military group.

SEIZING POWER

A coup (short for coup d'état) is an unconstitutional act, breaking the agreed rules of how a country is governed. The chief characteristic of a coup is that power is seized from above—by people who already hold some power—rather than changing hands with people's agreement in a democratic process. In a coup, change is often brought about by physical force or the threat of violence and may result in the military or a dictator (a ruler with total power over a country) replacing the existing government.

MILITARY TAKEOVER

No such goal inspired the wave of coups that toppled governments in South and Central America during the Cold War of the 1950s onward, when Western powers feared the global spread of communism.

In 1976, for example, Argentina's military overthrew the government of Isabel Péron. The "junta" (a Spanish term for a military group that rules after seizing power) suspended all political activity. Under the right-wing dictatorship that followed, many thousands of Argentinians were "disappeared" or killed before democracy was restored in 1983.

Coups have toppled many of the post-colonial governments of African countries, too, some of them repeatedly. More than 80 successful coups have taken place in the

48 states of sub-Saharan Africa since they gained independence. As recently as 2017, the Zimbabwean military ousted Robert Mugabe from power, in what it insisted was not a military takeover but was clearly a coup.

EMERGENCY POWERS

During a crisis that threatens the state and people's lives, a democratic government may exercise its right to act outside the constitution, using what are known as "emergency powers." In times of war, natural disaster, or a threat to democracy such as an act of terrorism, the constitution may be suspended and replaced by these temporary powers. In the US, for example, the president has the power to call a "national emergency" and then exceed many of the legal limits of their authority to do such things as closing borders. However, these powers expire after a year, and must be justified to Congress within six months.

ABUSE OF POWER

In a coup, the military or another group may abuse these emergency powers in order to seize control. Suspending the constitution that sets out the rules and powers of government, and acting outside the law, gives coup leaders the power to act as they please. Silencing the media, detaining citizens without trial, and banning travel—all this and more may be done on the pretext of "protecting" the people or "restoring stability," or in reality to suppress opposition.

Even with legal safeguards, suspending a constitution under emergency powers is risky—instead of protecting citizens, it may lead to a loss of their rights. Having seen emergency powers in the 1930s give rise to Adolf Hitler and the Holocaust, post-war Germany defined their use but is determined not to invoke them again.

People
POWER

FREE SPEECH is...

THE MEDIA is...

ACTIVISM is...

Che Guevara

ENVIRONMENTALISM is...

Climate strike

FEMINISM is...

Votes for women

MULTICULTURALISM is...

TERRORISM is...

REVOLUTION is...

The Arab Spring

HOW CAN I GET INVOLVED?

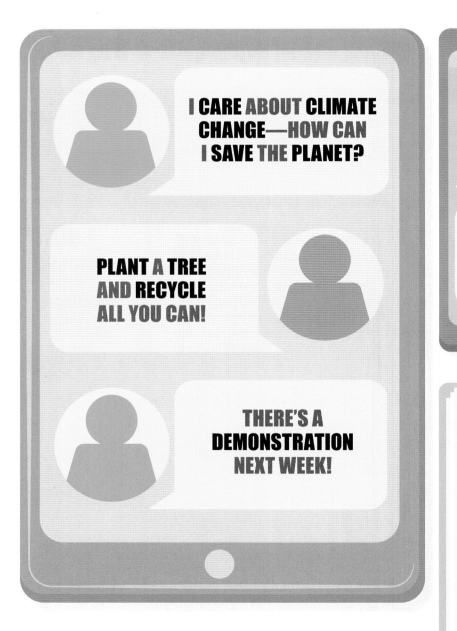

I CARE ABOUT CLIMATE CHANGE—HOW CAN I SAVE THE PLANET?

PLANT A TREE AND RECYCLE ALL YOU CAN!

THERE'S A DEMONSTRATION NEXT WEEK!

ARE HUMAN RIGHTS WORTH FIGHTING FOR?

POWER TO THE PEOPLE!

ARE VIOLENT PROTESTS EVER JUSTIFIED?

DO NONVIOLENT DEMONSTRATIONS WORK?

We are faced with choices every day: perhaps we have to choose between speaking up about an issue that we feel strongly about—or deciding not to take action.

When we speak up, we may not change the world, but we can make a difference. People power works! Whether we want to challenge our local store to reduce plastic or campaign for a government to pass a law, there are many ways we can voice our opinions and be heard. We can join a pressure group, a protest march, or political party. We can sign a petition, post a hashtag, boycott an organization because of unethical practices, or vote in an election. Politics is everywhere, and all these actions are political. Moreover, with growing online activism between people in many different countries, we can make a difference to global politics, not just to our local communities.

I WANT TO MAKE A DIFFERENCE!

HOW DO I GET MY LOCAL POLITICIAN TO LISTEN?

ARE REVOLUTIONS STILL HAPPENING?

SHOULD WE BE ALLOWED TO EXPRESS ANY OPINION?

I SUPPORT DIVERSITY, BUT IS MULTICULTURALISM WORKING?

CAN ANYONE BE A FEMINIST?

CAN WE TRUST WHAT WE READ ON SOCIAL MEDIA?

> ## "If liberty means anything at all, it means the right to tell people what they do not want to hear."
> GEORGE ORWELL (1903–1950)
> British writer and journalist

FREE SPEECH is...

THE RIGHT TO EXPRESS OPINIONS WITHOUT GOVERNMENT RESTRAINT, RETALIATION, OR CENSORSHIP

Freedom of speech is an ideal that dates back to ancient Greece, when citizens of the Athenian democracy (507–322 BCE) were free to discuss politics openly. The right to free speech was also a key demand championed in the French Revolution of 1789.

In 1948 the United Nations (UN) made a Universal Declaration of Human Rights, which stated: "Everyone has the right to freedom of opinion and expression." Most democratic nations agree that free speech applies to every medium of communication, as stipulated by the UN. Today, the internet, with over 4.5 billion users, has provided a wide platform for expression, but has also created new challenges as society debates whether there is a line over which controversial speech is not acceptable.

THE HARM PRINCIPLE
The 19th-century English philosopher John Stuart Mill wrote about "the harm principle," stating that free speech that causes harm to others is not truly free at all—it is an illusion of freedom. In the modern world, a much cited example of how free speech can be harmful is online "trolling." "Troll" is the slang term for a person who starts arguments on the internet with the aim of provoking individuals or groups—they are bullies who hide behind anonymity. Their "hate speech" can stir up hostility that intimidates or silences the voices of their victims.

CAUSING OFFENSE
On January 7, 2015, two Islamic extremist gunmen entered the Paris offices of *Charlie Hebdo*, a French satirical magazine that ridicules topics of a political or societal nature. The gunmen murdered 12 of the magazine's employees. The storming was in

reprisal for the magazine's publication of cartoons featuring Prophet Muhammad, whose depiction is forbidden in many interpretations of Islam. The attack was condemned worldwide for its violence but opened up debate over whether certain types of freedom of expression should be limited by law because they are provocative or offensive to some people.

CENSORSHIP

Censorship is the process of imposing checks and regulations on a person's right to free speech. It can be viewed as a curb on a person's liberty, but some people see it as necessary to protect the wider community's human rights. An example of this might be the censorship of state classified information, which is held secret, arguably in the interest of a population's security. Another type of censorship was prompted by the 2019 terrorist attack on a mosque in Christchurch, New Zealand. The alleged perpetrator's racist and anti-immigrant manifesto was published online at the time of the attacks, but it has since been declared objectionable by New Zealand's chief censor, meaning possession or distribution of it is illegal. In some circumstances, state censorship is taken much further. In countries such as China, the government tightly regulates internet content to limit people's access to information that might jeopardize its authority. In North Korea, there is no free media and people are not allowed to express opinion that is critical of its leader Kim Jong-un.

CONTROVERSY

Campaigners for free speech argue that it is vital for everyone to have their say in order to have healthy debate. They also think that censorship can be counterproductive, leading people to express their opinions in underhand or violent ways. The US is against banning hate speech, citing the 1791 First Amendment to the US Constitution. In Germany, however, where the Nazis rose to power in the 1930s through harmful rhetoric, hate speech can carry a prison sentence. The concept of free speech is constantly being challenged, debated, and updated.

IBERTY

REEDOM

OPINION

> ## "The moment we no longer have a free press, anything can happen."
> ### HANNAH ARENDT (1906–1975)
> German-American political theorist

THE MEDIA is...

THE MANY FORMS OF MASS COMMUNICATION THAT KEEP PEOPLE INFORMED AND HOLD THOSE IN POWER TO ACCOUNT

The media plays a vital role in politics. In a democracy, it informs people of the facts about a wide range of topics and issues, and provides a vehicle for all voices to be heard. This helps to hold politicians to account.

POLITICAL INFLUENCE

In the 1900s, the media expanded from newspapers to radio, film, and television. Print and broadcast media became known as the "mass media," which played an increasing role in politics because it reached vast audiences.

Where there is a "free press," the media is free to report on all news and current events and can express any opinions, even if these criticize the government. An unrestrained media can challenge leaders, probe government policies and decisions, and expose corruption or unethical behavior from politicians. Investigative reporting, in particular, can unearth facts that governments try to hide, such as atrocities carried out by the US military in the Vietnam War (1955–1975), which were exposed by US journalist Seymour Hersh in 1969. Such exposés can shape a nation's actions.

The media has always been used by politicians to manipulate public opinion. When it is not free, it can be a powerful tool for propaganda and control. In 1933, the Nazi regime in Germany deployed radio, press, and newsreels (films of the news shown in movie theaters) to stoke fears of a communist uprising, then used the public's anxieties to bring in political measures that eradicated civil liberties and democracy.

NEW MEDIA

In the past, it could take hours or days for news to travel. The internet now spreads information instantly, radically altering the way people engage with politics. Most people now get their news information online. While this may be from the digital versions of traditional media, it is increasingly from social media platforms such as Facebook and Twitter. Politicians around the world have therefore invested heavily in social media, using it to affirm their political beliefs, advertise, and win support during elections. Champions of social media suggest that sharing news on these platforms has led to an increased dialogue between politicians and the electorate. However, the rise of the internet has led to concerns that information published online— untethered from the journalistic ethics that to some extent govern broadcast and print media— is becoming more sensationalist and biased. Moreover, internet forums can create "echo chambers" that confirm their audiences' prejudices, adding instability to communications.

FAKE NEWS

One of the main concerns about unregulated news online is the growth of "fake news." This refers to made-up facts and misinformation that can spread fast via social media and sway views. Once established in the collective mind, these false facts are hard to contradict, even if disproved.

In 2019, Brazil elected a new, far-right, populist president, Jair Bolsonaro. During his campaign, a disinformation campaign on WhatsApp (the messaging app owned by Facebook) put out untrue and damaging stories about his left-wing opponent. These played a role in the victory of Bolsonaro's illiberal regime.

There are allegations, too, that some authoritarian states, such as China and Russia, have manipulated social media to destabilize democracies abroad.

Amid the overload of information online, there are increasing calls for self-regulation by internet companies. Telling a reliable and relevant story is more important than ever. At the same time, ever more schools are teaching the media literacy skills that will help students to distinguish fact from fiction and to recognize bias in the media.

> "Our lives begin to end the day we stay silent about things that matter."
> MARTIN LUTHER KING, JR. (1929–1968)
> American church minister and civil-rights activist

ACTIVISM is...

THE USE OF DIRECT ACTION TO HIGHLIGHT AN ISSUE IN ORDER TO BRING ABOUT SOCIAL OR POLITICAL CHANGE

History has been shaped by those who have taken a stand and fought for change. Some of the biggest shifts in society have come about as a result of activism—the direct campaigning of individuals or groups to fight for causes they feel passionate about.

PRESSING ISSUES
Action can be taken to support local, national, or international causes. An example of a local issue might be the closure of a hospital, which affects a community's quality of life. Local activism can involve writing letters to politicians, door-to-door campaigning, attending public meetings, or handing out leaflets. On a national level, people may take action over issues such as taxes, corruption, or a country's decision to go to war. They join marches, strikes, or sign petitions to express their opinions. Global issues concerning people today include gender inequality, racism, and climate change. Demonstrations are sometimes held on the same day in several worldwide locations.

ACTIVIST GROUPS
Many activists are volunteers who join interest or pressure groups—organizations that run campaigns and lobby governments to influence the laws that get passed. In international groups, such as the environmental organization World Wide Fund for Nature, or the human rights body Amnesty International, volunteers work together with paid staff to try to achieve the groups' aims.

FREEDOM OF ASSEMBLY

For centuries, in moments of civil discontent, people have taken to the streets to demand change. In 1983, millions of supporters of the Campaign for Nuclear Disarmament (CND) demonstrated against the deployment of US nuclear missiles to sites in Western Europe during the arms race between the US and the Soviet Union. More recently, in 2018, the environmental movement Extinction Rebellion (XR) advocated nonviolent civil disobedience to urge governments to respond to the climate crisis. In London, some protesters blocked traffic and others glued themselves to a train.

VIOLENT CLASHES

Most democratic countries consider freedom of assembly, which is the right of individuals to gather and protest with others, to be a basic human right. However, many governments, especially in authoritarian states, place limits on people's rights to protest, if the protests are perceived as a threat to their power. Governments may also shut down demonstrations if they fear violence, but an aggressive response can make violence worse. For example, in 2019 in Hong Kong, clashes erupted between protesters and police during antigovernment demonstrations.

ONLINE ACTIVISM

Today, social media has enabled activists to amass in vast numbers quickly. In so-called "hashtag activism" people use Twitter hashtags (#) to express their opinions, and to sign online petitions, write political blogs, lobby governments with emails, and start social-media campaigns, all of which rapidly thrust issues into the public consciousness. During the September 2019 protests to demand action against climate change, many students skipped school to take part. They then posted about it on social media, drawing more people into the movement.

Che Guevara

1928–1967

Marxist revolutionary Ernesto "Che" Guevara was an Argentinian medical graduate who fiercely committed himself to the socialist cause in 1950s Latin America. Joining the rebel army of legendary Cuban leader Fidel Castro, Guevara fought in the guerrilla campaign that toppled Cuba's then dictatorship. In Castro's newly formed government, Guevara became not only a powerful figurehead in Cuba but a world-famous icon of the left.

> ## "The revolution is not an apple that falls when it's ripe. You have to make it fall."

Growing awareness

Born into a middle-class family in Rosário, Argentina, Che Guevara studied medicine in Buenos Aires. As a student he traveled by motorcycle across South and Central America, where the widespread poverty and inequality overwhelmed him with anger. In Guatemala, where he witnessed a US-backed military coup destroy hopes of much-needed land reforms, Guevara became convinced that only force would bring justice. In 1954, he found a cause that changed the course of his life when he met Cuban revolutionary Fidel Castro and his brother Raúl in Mexico City. Sharing the same ideals, they plotted to topple Cuba's dictator Fulgencio Batista, launching their first attack with a small guerrilla force carried by boat.

Che the rebel fighter

During the guerrilla warfare that followed in the Sierra Maestra mountains of Cuba, Guevara—now nicknamed "Che"—developed into a ruthless fighter and skilled strategist. In 1959, the rebels seized control of the country, making Cuba a socialist state with Castro as president. Che held various positions in the government. He is said to have had a dark side, and allegedly oversaw the executions of hundreds of political prisoners.

Violent end

In 1965, disenchanted by Cuba's tightening links with the Soviet Union, Che left to start fresh revolutions. Attempting a coup in Bolivia, he was taken by the Bolivian army and shot on October 9, 1967. He was 39. In 1997, bodies thought to be those of Che and the guerrillas who died with him were found in Bolivia. Returned to Cuba, they lie buried in Santa Clara, honored by a vast memorial.

Che and Castro
Trusted aide of Fidel Castro (right), Che Guevara was a hero of the victorious Cuban Revolution in 1959. He was a key figure in Castro's government for a time, but in the mid-1960s left Cuba to fight in other wars.

Poster boy
This iconic photograph of Che Guevara, taken in 1960 and titled "Heroic guerrilla fighter," is still a powerful symbol of revolution. Printed on posters and mass-produced goods such as T-shirts, the image sold in the millions.

> "There can be no plan B because there is no planet B."
> BAN KI-MOON (born 1944)
> Former United Nations secretary general

ENVIRONMENTALISM is...

A POLITICAL, SOCIAL, AND ETHICAL MOVEMENT THAT SEEKS TO PROTECT THE ENVIRONMENT FROM DAMAGE CAUSED BY HUMAN ACTIVITY

As Earth moves toward a global population of eight billion, there is now a consensus that human activity is changing the climate. One of Earth's main life-support systems, the climate determines whether or not humans and other plant and animal species can live on the planet. This and other, often related, environmental issues such as pollution, plastic waste, and threats to biodiversity, have placed environmentalism at the top of the political agenda.

WATERSHED MOMENT

Today's environmental movement grew from the publication in 1962 of *Silent Spring*, written by American biologist Rachel Carson. In it, Carson exposed the harmful effects of the chemical pesticide DDT on plant and animal life.

The book represented a watershed moment, making links between pollution and public health and raising public awareness and concern for the environment. Carson showed that humans and the rest of the natural world were all part of a single ecosystem (a network of living organisms). In doing so, Carson made it clear that people had to think ecologically.

GREEN POLITICS

In the 1970s, some environmentalists thought that environmental issues could only be addressed within a political and economic framework. The world's first "green" party, the United Tasmania Party, was formed in 1972 to oppose the construction of a dam in Australia. From 1993, *Die Grünen* (the Greens in Germany) thrust green politics further into the limelight, entering electoral politics and winning seats in the German parliament. Green parties emerged in other countries to support conservation and the environment and became united in an international network of political parties and movements. They are largely considered left of the political spectrum and tend to be rooted in nonviolence, social justice, and grassroots democracy (action by all). Now an established force in politics, green parties have so far not had the power to make the deep changes environmentalists demand.

PLANET-SIZED ISSUES

The alarming pace of climate change combined with degradation of the environment by, for instance, deforestation and air pollution have pushed green politics to the fore. Experts warn that, without taking steps to protect the planet, there will be more natural disasters such as floods, droughts, tropical storms, and wildfires.

In 2015, the threat of climate change had become so immediate that world leaders met in Paris, France to agree a deal to reduce the greenhouse gas emissions that trap heat in Earth's atmosphere. Negotiations were fraught, as developing (third-world) countries such as India argued that developed (first-world) nations should take responsibility for their historic emissions by contributing funds and new technologies to developing countries. Despite this, most of the 196 nations did adopt the world's first legally binding global climate deal, the Paris Agreement. Since then, many environmentalists have accused world leaders of being too slow to meet the deal's targets.

CALL TO ACTION

Outside of party politics, environmental activism refers to the coming together of various groups and organizations that collaborate in social, scientific, political, and conservation fields to address environmental concerns. Lobbying and pressure groups, such as Friends of the Earth (formed 1969) and Greenpeace (1971), advocate for new legislation and keep environmental issues in the headlines.

Youth activists have also called on world leaders to do more on environmental issues, and the world is paying attention. Inspired by teenage activist Greta Thunberg from Sweden, young people have become politically engaged and inspired to make changes in their behavior to protect the environment. Individuals have given up waiting for governments to act. They are using less single-use plastic, reducing waste, and traveling responsibly to try to ensure that the next generation, and the planet, have a safe future.

"Change is coming, whether you like it or not."

GRETA THUNBERG (born 2003)
Swedish environmental activist

CLIMATE STRIKE

since AUGUST 2018

When 15-year-old Greta Thunberg sat outside the Swedish parliament to protest against climate change, instead of going to school, her solo strike went viral. It raised awareness and sparked a global youth movement.

Greta Thunberg was horrified by people's lack of action on climate change. When she held her first *Skolstrejk för klimatet* ("School strike for the climate") one Friday in August 2018, her objective was to pressurize the Swedish government to fulfil its obligations to the Paris Agreement. This was a set of targets agreed to by 197 countries in 2016 to stop the global temperature from rising more than 3.6°F (2°C) above the levels recorded in the 1800s, before the Industrial Revolution. Such a catastrophic rise in temperature is now seen as a potential climate emergency.

Inspired by Thunberg's conviction and positive action, young people around the world skipped school and started their own climate strikes, posting photos on social media with the hashtags #Fridaysforfuture and #Climatestrike. In September 2019, an estimated six million people in 150 countries took part in the first Global Week for Future, a series of climate strikes.

Thunberg and other climate strikers argue that, although their education is important, there is no point in going to school if our planet has no future. They need adults, and especially global leaders, to take note and then take action.

Global concern
Young activists in Kiev, Ukraine, demand action on global warming in September 2019 as part of the Global Week for Future climate-strike protests.

> "A feminist is anyone who recognizes the equality and full humanity of women and men."
> GLORIA STEINEM (born 1934)
> American second-wave feminist and political activist

FEMINISM is...

THE BELIEF THAT MEN AND WOMEN SHOULD HAVE EQUAL RIGHTS AND EQUAL OPPORTUNITIES, AND THE ADVOCACY OF WOMEN'S RIGHTS

SEE ALSO:
← Human rights
pages 76-77
← Suffrage
pages 88-89
← Activism
pages 104-105

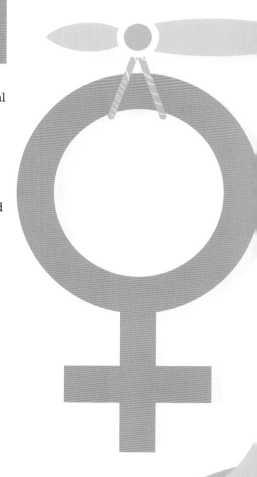

Feminism is a political and social movement that challenges the way in which women and girls are treated because they are female. Feminist history is often described in "waves." Until the late 1800s, most women were not educated, were unable to vote, and their property or earnings usually belonged to their fathers or husbands. In the first wave of feminism, in the 19th and early 20th century, suffragists fought for women's rights to own property and to vote. New Zealand was the first country to allow women the vote, in 1893.

NOT JUST THE VOTE
The second wave of feminism, which reached its height in the 1970s and 1980s, refers to the Women's Liberation Movement,

which pushed for further reform, such as gender equality in pay and liberalized divorce laws. It also sought to give women more control over their bodies, campaigning for greater access to the contraceptive pill, and worked to protect women from domestic violence. Second-wave feminism raised awareness of the idea that society has historically been a patriarchy—a society in which men hold the power, be it within the family, government, work, education, or religion—and that sexist power politics influence many aspects of women's lives.

In 1979, a United Nations (UN) international convention required nations to agree to end discrimination against women in all forms—though in practice this has proved difficult to enforce. While gender equality has made significant inroads in some countries, women in other nations, particularly in less developed regions, still fight for basic rights.

BROADENING APPEAL

Beginning in the 1990s, the third wave of feminism questioned and redefined ideas about gender stereotypes, womanhood, and sexuality. It sought to broaden its appeal to women of all cultural backgrounds and encourage them to define what feminism meant to them personally. It championed the idea that all women could be assertive and in control of their destinies, summed up by the 1990s phrase "girl power."

MODERN FEMINISM

A fourth wave of feminism emerged in the early 2010s. It raised awareness of sexual assault, harassment, and body-shaming—the practice of making critical comments about a person's body. It is characterized by "hashtag activism," the use of Twitter's hashtags (#) for internet activism. English writer Laura Bates's Everyday Sexism Project (2012) was an open forum where women could post their experiences of harassment. Tens of thousands of women from across the world responded. The use of social media has seen feminists mobilize through an explosion of blogs and viral videos.

In 2017, more than 80 women accused the US film producer Harvey Weinstein of sexual harassment. In response, the American actress Alyssa Milano suggested that anyone who had been "sexually harassed or assaulted" should reply to her Tweet with "#MeToo," resurrecting a movement started by US activist Tarana Burke in 2006. Half a million women responded in the first 24 hours, exposing the full extent of sexual harassment across the world. Due in part to this activism, France made catcalling a punishable offense in 2018 and the European Parliament convened a special session on sexual harassment.

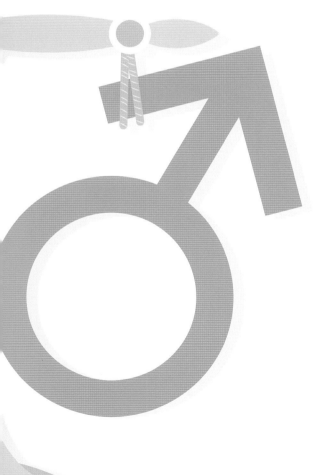

VOTES FOR WOMEN

October 1903–August 1914

In 1903, after decades of peaceful yet fruitless campaigning for women's right to vote, a new, militant women's suffrage organization was launched in Britain. This group played a major part in winning the vote for women.

Founded by Emmeline Pankhurst and her daughters, Christabel and Sylvia, the Women's Social and Political Union (WSPU) differed from previous women's suffrage organizations, which for half a century had campaigned for the vote using law-abiding methods. Known as suffragists, these women had relied on tactics such as petitions and letter-writing to obtain the vote, but with little success.

In contrast, the WSPU effectively declared war on the all-male parliament, determined to win the vote, as Pankhurst said, "by any means possible"—even if that meant breaking the law. Nicknamed "suffragettes," the WSPU adopted bold tactics, such as encouraging women to invade parliament. From 1905 to 1914, suffragettes were rarely out of the news, making votes for women a top political issue.

The official response was brutal. Women were attacked and at least 1,000 imprisoned. Some of these went on hunger strike, only to be cruelly force-fed. In 1913, the movement's first martyr was created when Emily Wilding Davison died after being trampled by the king's racehorse when she ran onto the racecourse at the Epsom Derby with a "votes for women" banner. Campaigning ended when war broke out in 1914, but some women got the vote in 1918.

Emmeline Pankhurst's arrest at a march in 1914
Faced with a government determined to withhold the vote from women, suffragettes attacked property and held suffrage marches. These were met with police brutality.

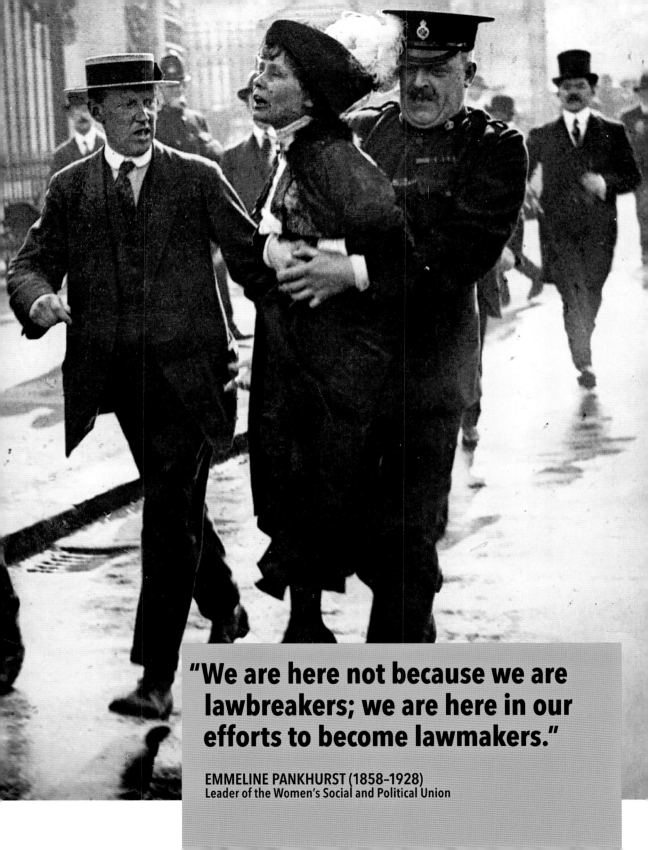

"We are here not because we are lawbreakers; we are here in our efforts to become lawmakers."

EMMELINE PANKHURST (1858–1928)
Leader of the Women's Social and Political Union

> "I define integration... as equal opportunity, accompanied by cultural diversity, in an atmosphere of mutual tolerance."
>
> ROY JENKINS (1920–2003)
> British politician

MULTICULTURALISM is...

A POLICY THAT AIMS TO SUPPORT THE DIFFERENT IDENTITIES AND CULTURES WITHIN A SOCIETY

SEE ALSO:

Human rights
pages 76–77

Nationalism
pages 132–133

Globalization
pages 142–143

The populations of most modern countries contain people from many diverse cultures and backgrounds. Over centuries, as people have moved from place to place in search of better economic opportunities, or to escape war or natural disasters, or as forced labor (slavery), societies have become more mixed. Multiculturalism as a policy attempts to deal with the challenges of building a stable society that incorporates many different identities.

BLENDING IN

Historically, migrants were encouraged to integrate into their new nation's dominant culture. In the 1800s, millions of Europeans moved to the US in search of a better life. They were expected to assimilate, or blend, into the great "melting pot" of American culture, to build a unified nation. The policy of assimilation has been justified on the grounds that it adheres to the liberal ideal that everyone should be treated equally, with no particular group receiving special treatment. Critics of assimilation argue that it has been used to suppress minority cultures.

THE SALAD BOWL

More recently, the idea that a nation thrives if its minority groups are able to preserve their traditions, languages, and cultures, has gained momentum. Canada, which for centuries has had French and English speakers and has attracted immigrants from all over the world, was one of the first nations to embrace cultural differences. In a speech to the Canadian Parliament in 1971, Prime Minister Pierre Elliott Trudeau stated, "A society which emphasizes uniformity is one which creates intolerance and hate." Since the 1970s other Western liberal democracies have implemented policies that promote the idea of society as a "salad bowl" with different ingredients forming a whole. Today, many governments have introduced legislation that supports this approach, such as laws that prohibit discrimination, promote the teaching of tolerance in schools, and celebrate the festivals of cultural minorities.

CHALLENGES

During the 2010s, unrest in Africa and the Middle East, including the civil war in Syria, forced millions of people to flee their countries. Many headed to the richer countries of Europe.

This "refugee crisis" challenged European governments to rethink multiculturalism. In 2010 German Chancellor Angela Merkel declared that multiculturalism had "utterly failed" because it had separated minority communities from the mainstream, creating greater potential for misunderstanding and distrust between the communities.

Others have argued that multiculturalism can be an obstacle to human rights. Some refugees come from countries that have more conservative views on women's rights and homosexuality than their host nations. Several European countries have placed restrictions on the Islamic practice of women wearing veils to cover their faces, on the grounds that it oppresses women.

The perception that immigration is increasing has also led some people to argue that the traditional identities of host nations are being diluted and that immigrants are a "burden" on a country's stretched resources, such as healthcare and welfare benefits. The result of this has been greater support for nationalist parties in host nations.

CULTURAL EXCHANGE

Countries that promote multiculturalism, such as Singapore, which has a very mixed population and many bilingual speakers, value the contribution that an influx of skills and foreign capital can bring to their economies. Businesses welcome multiculturalism; a diverse workforce, combined with modern technology, can generate business across borders. Moreover, multiculturalism forges a rich cultural exchange in attitudes to life and traditions, and encourages tolerance between different groups.

> "Terrorism has become the systematic weapon of a war that knows no borders or seldom has a face."
>
> JACQUES CHIRAC (1932–2019)
> Former president of France

TERRORISM is...

THE UNLAWFUL USE OF VIOLENCE, OR THE THREAT OF DEATH OR INJURY, DIRECTED IN PURSUIT OF, OR IN SERVICE OF, A POLITICAL AIM

SEE ALSO:

Shock waves were felt around the world when the 9/11 attacks took place in the US in 2001. This was when members of a militant Islamist organization known as al-Qaeda flew planes into the World Trade Center in New York and other US buildings, killing more than 3,000 people. It was the single deadliest terrorist act ever known.

SPREADING FEAR

Terrorism is considered to be any violent threat or action designed to influence a government or intimidate the public in order to bring political change. The word "terror" derives from the Latin *terrere*, meaning "to frighten." The aim of terrorism is to spread fear so that citizens feel unsafe and afraid to lead normal lives.

Terrorists may use bombs, guns, chemical weapons, kidnapping and hijacking—or even aircraft. They may operate solely within their own country, or across national borders (international terrorism).

Some governments have been accused of "state terrorism," too, either using violence against their own civilians, or conducting military actions beyond their own borders that have killed or injured civilians outside the normal rules of war. One example of this is the 1988 bombing in mid-air of Pan Am flight 103 by Libya, over Lockerbie in Scotland, killing a total of 270 people.

The use of violence as a political strategy of fear has been around for centuries, but terrorism today has a global impact as modern media give terrorist acts a higher profile.

A MEANS TO AN END

Terrorists and their supporters believe that violent actions are justified when carried out for political purposes, and in particular if they feel that there is no other way to achieve their objectives.

Nationalist groups fighting for liberation from colonial powers, such as the Mau Mau who rebelled against British rule in Kenya in the 1950s, have used terrorist tactics. Ethnic groups wanting to break away from a state may also give rise to terrorism. In 1959, separatist group ETA (Basque Country and Freedom) started a 60-year-long armed conflict against Spain to win independence for the Basque country.

Other groups have used terrorism to try and achieve broader political goals, such as FARC (the Revolutionary Armed Forces of Colombia), which fought for 50 years to overthrow the Colombian government and put a communist leadership in its place.

What is seen as legitimate resistance from one viewpoint can look like terrorism from another. Members of the African National Congress (ANC) party, who used guerrilla tactics in their fight for equality for black people in South Africa during apartheid (1948–1994), were labeled terrorists by the government. To their supporters, they were freedom fighters and their leader, Nelson Mandela, a national hero.

RADICALIZATION

Terrorist groups thrive in areas where people already hold strong views on political, social, or religious issues. They may recruit members through a process of radicalization, influencing individuals to adopt extreme views and commit violent acts. The fundamentalist terror group known as Islamic State (ISIS) has radicalized new members online through slick propaganda and the use of social media to target possible recruits. Many of these are young Muslims who feel left out by the societies in which they live.

NEW THREATS

In the 21st century, terrorism is changing. Recent years have seen the "lone wolf" become the world's most urgent terrorist threat. The term describes someone who acts alone and is not affiliated to a group. A solo terrorist is particularly hard for national security services to track down. Lone far-right terrorists have emerged as a major threat in the US. These include the gunman who, in August 2019, killed 22 people at a Walmart store in El Paso, Texas. Before his attack, the man had posted a manifesto online promoting white nationalist views and fostering distrust of other ethnic groups.

Cyberterrorism—the politically motivated use of computers and the internet to disrupt civilian life —is also a significant terrorist threat. States fear that cyberterrorists might be able to cripple their armed forces, shut down the electricity grid, or even blow up a nuclear reactor.

Global measures to counter terrorism are sophisticated, using international data to track and disable terrorist movements. However, such moves can also be seen as a means for governments to clamp down on their political opponents.

> ## "Power concedes nothing without a demand. It never did and it never will."
> **FREDERICK DOUGLASS (1818–1895)**
> African American writer and social reformer

REVOLUTION is...

A MOVEMENT BY THE PEOPLE TO OVERTHROW AN EXISTING POLITICAL REGIME, SOMETIMES BY FORCE

The word "revolution" most often refers to the forceful removal of a government, either to replace it with a new governing system or to gain independence from another country. For centuries, it is revolution that has brought about the most radical change in the political order of society.

FUNDAMENTAL CHANGE

Resistance and rebellion both involve opposition to political authority, but revolution brings about a fundamental change in power, transforming the way a society functions.

While the means of every revolution may be the same, the desired ends of each can be very different. One of the earliest revolutions in modern history was the American Revolution (1775–1783), which resulted in the US declaring itself independent from Britain. Its ideas of liberty and political autonomy inspired the French Revolution (1789–1799), when ordinary people rose up against the aristocracy.

In the 1900s, the Russian Revolution (1917–1923) sent shock waves around the world. Inspired by Marxism, it aimed to create a more equal society by eradicating social classes. The revolution ended the rule of the Tsarist monarchy, ultimately replacing it with a communist state, the Soviet Union, led by Lenin until his death in 1924.

The rule of the Communist Party in China was established after two revolutions. In October 1911, a group of revolutionaries led a revolt against the imperial Qing Dynasty, establishing a republic in its place. This was the first step in a process of upheaval completed by the 1949 revolution, when communist leader Mao Zedong entered Beijing and declared the creation of the People's Republic of China (PRC).

In 1979, the Iranian Revolution led to Iran's monarchy under Shah Mohammed Reza Pahlavi being ousted. It was replaced with an Islamic republic led by cleric Ayatollah Khomeini.

GENTLE REVOLUTION

When people challenge the status quo in order to bring about political change, they are liable to face violent repression from the ruling authority. People may be willing to give their lives to get rid of oppressive regimes, even with no guarantees that the new regime will be better, so revolutions throughout history have been associated with bloodshed and violence.

However, not all revolutions are bloody and violent. The citizens of some countries have tried to overturn a regime using violent tactics and then, when the time was ripe, successfully adopted nonviolent strategies. In 1989, as the Soviet Union loosened its grip on Eastern Europe, Czechoslovakia staged a revolution that became known as the Velvet Revolution. This peaceful uprising involved demonstrations and strikes by the people. It ended communist rule in the country and saw the election of its first democratically elected president in decades, playwright-turned-dissident Václav Havel.

LEADERLESS REVOLUTION

In 2011, a series of uprisings known as the Arab Spring broke out across the Middle East and North Africa. The protests, which were organized via social media with no obvious leaders, led to regime changes in some countries, such as Egypt and Tunisia. However, there was no clear consensus on the desired outcome of the revolutions. In some countries, this state of uncertainty created a political vacuum, allowing repressive leaders and groups to take charge. Other countries descended into chaos and civil war. Not all revolutions succeed, but they continue to make history today.

THE ARAB SPRING

SPRING 2011

In 2011, a series of uprisings calling for political freedom swept through the Arab world. Tired of poverty, corruption, and repression, thousands of people joined protests as word spread via social media.

The Arab Spring began in Tunisia with one man. When Mohamed Bouazizi had his vegetable cart confiscated by police, he set himself on fire. His desperate act, in December 2010, sparked a firestorm that raced across North Africa and the Middle East.

The scale of the uprising was unexpected. Presidents who had held power for decades were removed and governments fell in Tunisia, Egypt, Libya, and Yemen. News of the dramatic events traveled fast, with protests, such as the huge gathering of activists in Tahrir Square in Cairo, Egypt, being organized via Facebook and other social media.

The countries affected were quick to quell rebellions through brutal crackdowns, though some offered political changes. Egypt held elections for a new leader, but soon underwent a military coup. Libya became a lawless place controlled by armed militias. Yemen's security forces responded violently and the country's leader was forced to step down. Syria's powerful regime withstood the protests and the unrest escalated into civil war.

The Arab Spring gave many people hopes of a rapid democratic change; but building a stable political structure in its wake has proved to be a slow and precarious business.

Egypt revolts
A protestor flourishes the Egyptian flag in Tahrir Square, Cairo, during fiery clashes between military forces and demonstrators in December 2011.

"The Arab Awakening, or Arab Spring, has transformed the geopolitical landscape."

BAN KI-MOON (born 1944)
Former United Nations secretary general

INTERNATIONAL
relations

IMPERIALISM is...

Mahatma Gandhi

NATIONALISM is...

Catalan separatism

GEOPOLITICS is...

WAR is...

The Iraq War

GLOBALIZATION is...

Rohingya migration

INTERNATIONAL ORGANIZATIONS are...

DOES POLITICS CROSS BORDERS?

IS COLONIALISM STILL RELEVANT TODAY?

WHAT IS THE UNITED NATIONS FOR?

WHY ARE SOME GLOBAL COMPANIES WEALTHIER THAN NATIONS?

IS GLOBALIZATION GOOD FOR US?

WHAT MAKES A NATION POWERFUL?

HOW DO WE TACKLE CLIMATE CHANGE TOGETHER?

Politics is not just about what's going on in our own countries, it's also about global issues. Our governments' decisions are often influenced by worldwide events.

Climate change, migration, poverty, disease, and trade deals are all examples of global challenges that can only be addressed if nations act together to find solutions. Moreover, our lives are increasingly shaped by globalization—the growth of large international companies and technological innovation that has made cultures, economics, and politics cross borders as never before.

International politics is often about resolving conflict between nations. There have always been disputes over territory, resources, or opposing religious or political beliefs, and some have led to war. The United Nations and other global organizations work to promote peace and cooperation and to improve everyone's lives, regardless of nationality, race, or religion.

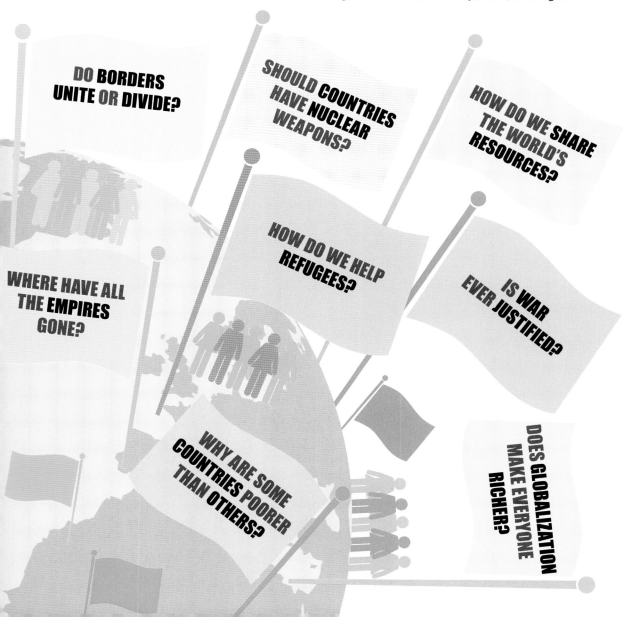

DO BORDERS UNITE OR DIVIDE?

SHOULD COUNTRIES HAVE NUCLEAR WEAPONS?

HOW DO WE SHARE THE WORLD'S RESOURCES?

WHERE HAVE ALL THE EMPIRES GONE?

HOW DO WE HELP REFUGEES?

IS WAR EVER JUSTIFIED?

WHY ARE SOME COUNTRIES POORER THAN OTHERS?

DOES GLOBALIZATION MAKE EVERYONE RICHER?

> "Veni, vidi, vici." ("I came, I saw, I conquered.")
> JULIUS CAESAR (100–44 BCE)
> Roman dictator, politician, and military general

IMPERIALISM is...

THE POLICY OF EXTENDING A COUNTRY'S RULE OVER FOREIGN NATIONS AND PEOPLES, OFTEN BY MILITARY FORCE

The word "imperialism" comes from the Latin *imperium*, which means "supreme power." Although empires have been in existence since ancient times, imperialism came into use as a political term in the 1870s, when it was used to describe the overseas policies of the UK. Today, the practice of imperialism is prohibited by international law.

EMPIRE AND COLONY

Imperialism and colonialism are two different, although related, things. Imperialism is the policy of conquering another nation's lands in order to increase dominance and create an empire. Colonialism, on the other hand, is the construction and maintenance of an outpost, or colony, populated by people coming from the home state.

Imperialism is a state policy, and is developed for both ideological and commercial reasons. Colonialism is more simply the creation of overseas colonies for settlement and trade. An empire, can, however, contain colonies.

There is also sometimes a difference in the geography. The Russian empire (1721–1917) and Ottoman empire (*ca.*1300–1922) were vast, continuous land masses. Colonies, however, are often distant and separated from the rest of the empire by sea.

Both imperialism and colonialism often include the use of force to gain control over foreign territories. The rulers of lands that become part of an empire are sometimes allowed to stay in power, provided that they recognize the emperor or monarch (or other ruler of the imperial state) as the sovereign. Colonies, on the other hand, are ruled directly.

DECOLONIZATION

Between the 15th and 20th centuries, European powers built huge empires in the Americas, Africa, and Asia. For the most part, imperial rule was deeply resented by the peoples in conquered lands. The process of relinquishing imperial control and granting dependent territories independence—known as "decolonization"—has often been difficult. The Vietnamese and Algerians fought major wars against the French in the 1950s and 1960s to win their independence from the French empire. During the same period, Britain was involved in colonial wars in Malaya, Aden, Kenya, and elsewhere. Few empires collapse peacefully.

NEOCOLONIALISM

Some empires control another country through economic or cultural domination, without ever ruling it directly, in a process known as "neocolonialism" or "neoimperialism." In the 1800s, Britain controlled three-fifths of all Argentinian investment and owned all of its railroads, even though Argentina was an independent state and never part of the British empire. Today, the US, China, Russia, and the EU exert huge global economic, cultural, and political influence, and are sometimes described as "empires." The term "neocolonialism" is also used in relation to the economic power that more developed countries and global businesses and institutions have over less developed countries.

POSTCOLONIAL IDEAS

Historically, rulers of empires have sought to justify their policies by arguing that imperialism has extended education, new technology, and other benefits to the people it has incorporated into their realms. But imperialism has always had its opponents. The Soviet communist leader Lenin (1870–1924) saw imperialism as being the highest or most advanced form of capitalism, bringing great wealth to those that had invested in it, but at the expense of the territories under their control. Today, the acceptance of the ideals of democracy and national sovereignty mean that imperialism is now considered a form of oppression and exploitation.

Mahatma Gandhi

1869–1848

Mohandas Karamchand Gandhi, known as Mahatma, meaning "great soul," used peaceful protest to campaign for India's independence from British colonial rule. Vowing to fight what he called the disease of color prejudice, Gandhi adopted the religious principle of *ahimsa* ("doing no harm") and turned it into a nonviolent tool for nationalist action.

> "I regard myself as a soldier, though a soldier of peace."

Finding his place

Born in 1869 in Porbandar, India, Gandhi trained as a lawyer in London before moving to South Africa. He lived there for 21 years, meeting the racial prejudices that led him into activism. Thrown off a train for traveling first class, he had a "moment of truth," shocked by the denial of his human rights. It was in South Africa that he first led nonviolent protests against racial injustice, for which he was imprisoned several times.

Return to India

In 1915, Gandhi returned to India, at a time when the country was increasingly unsettled under British rule. In 1919, the British government passed an act allowing the imprisonment without trial of suspected terrorists. Gandhi urged nonviolent protest or *satyagraha* ("devotion to truth") against this obvious attempt to increase British power. The trigger for stronger protests came when British soldiers fired on a peaceful demonstration in the city of Amritsar, killing hundreds. In the wake of the massacre, Gandhi launched a nationwide campaign of noncooperation with the British.

Toward independence

Elected leader of the Indian National Congress party in 1920, Gandhi was a key figure in Indian politics over the following decades, his protests earning him spells in prison. Despite his pleas for peace, he was often unable to prevent civil unrest turning into violence. Dedicated to breaking down barriers between castes and faiths, Gandhi was deeply saddened by the riots that broke out between Hindus and Muslims when India became independent in 1947. A year later, Gandhi was shot and killed by a Hindu extremist.

The Salt March
In 1930, in protest against a tax the British had imposed on salt, Gandhi walked 241 miles (388 km) to the sea to make his own salt. Tens of thousands of people joined him along the way, including Indian poet and activist Sarojini Naidu (above).

Humble leader
Gandhi believed in the simple life. He rejected modern industrialization and encouraged people to use traditional skills. In later life, he chose to dress in the cotton shawl and loincloth worn by the poorest of his fellow citizens.

> **"Patriotism is when love of your own people comes first; nationalism, when hate for people other than your own comes first."**
> CHARLES DE GAULLE (1890–1970)
> Leader of the French Resistance and former president of France

NATIONALISM is...

SUPPORT FOR AND LOYALTY TO A NATION, SOMETIMES IN A WAY THAT IS HARMFUL TO THE INTERESTS OF OTHER NATIONS

Nationalism is one of the most important political ideas of the last two centuries. It has created new nations and broken up old empires, redrawing the map of the world. It has caused people to view themselves and their countries in a new light. Nationalism itself is based on two assumptions: that humankind is naturally divided into distinct nations of similar people, and that the nation state is the most appropriate and legitimate unit of political rule.

DOCTRINE OR IDEOLOGY?

Nationalism can be seen as a doctrine—a set of beliefs—or as an ideology—a system of ideals. As a doctrine, nationalism states that all nations are entitled to be independent and to govern themselves, and that the world should consist of entirely self-governing nation states. As an ideology, however, nationalism goes much further, promoting a belief in patriotism or support for one's country. It also promotes political, cultural, and ethnic identity, placing one's own nation above every other nation, possibly to the other nation's detriment.

NATIONAL IDENTITY

As both a doctrine and an ideology, nationalism has great strengths. It can bring a people together and give them a common identity. But nationalism also has a darker side. By stressing the racial unity of a country, nationalism can lead to racism against minority peoples within that country. It can also lead to xenophobia, a dislike of or prejudice against people from other countries. Above all, in promoting intense national enthusiasm, it can give birth to movements such as Fascism or Nazism, both of which were fanatically nationalist.

SHAPING HISTORY

Nationalism had a huge impact in 19th-century Europe. Italians came together to create a new, united nation, Germans also formed a unified state, and the Irish began their long struggle to gain freedom from British rule.

In the 1900s, World War II (1939–1945) was to a large extent caused by the militaristic policies of nationalist regimes, such as those of Germany and Japan, and their invasion of other nations in order to expand their borders. After the war, Indian nationalists won independence from British colonial rule in 1947, and nationalities across the Middle East and Africa also gained their independence from former European empires.

In 1991, nationalism contributed to the break-up of the Soviet Union, a state formed in 1922 of federal republics. A period of reforms in the 1980s aimed at liberalizing the economy and structure of the Soviet Union's centralized Communist government in Moscow, led to a wave of revolutions and eventually the formation of 15 independent states. In the 21st century, growing nationalist sentiment in the largest of these states, Russia, has helped its government, led by Vladimir Putin, to justify the annexation of the neighboring region of Crimea from Ukraine. Nationalism is considered to be on the rise in the 21st century. Some present-day nationalist groups are associated with religion. Hindu nationalists in India and Buddhist groups in Myanmar, Thailand, and Sri Lanka, are seeking to instil religious principles at the heart of government rule.

SEPARATISM

Many states of the world contain more than one regional identity. Spain contains both Basque and Catalan people, for example, and Canada both English and French speakers. Problems arise when these minority peoples wish to separate from the state and become independent nations themselves. In the UK, Scotland held a referendum in 2014 on whether to become an independent nation, narrowly deciding to remain. Catalonia held an illegal referendum in 2017 on whether to leave Spain, then illegally declared itself an independent republic. In the Middle East, the Kurds are a people that live in a mountainous territory straddling the borders of Turkey, Iraq, Syria, and Iran. They have taken up arms in a fight for independence, but their struggle has repeatedly been suppressed. The Kurds remain the biggest single ethnic group in the world yet to gain their own state.

"The welfare of Catalonia is only possible outside of Spain."

CARLES PUIGDEMONT (born 1962)
Former president of the Parliament of Catalonia

CATALAN SEPARATISM

OCTOBER 2017

Catalonia is a prosperous region of Spain with 7.5 million people and its own identity, language, and parliament. Since the birth of Spain in 1512, the question of whether Catalonia should be an independent nation has divided both the region and the country.

After an illegal referendum in 2017, the Catalan parliament took the matter into its own hands, declaring independence for the region and plunging Spain into political crisis.

In 2010, the Spanish government had taken away some powers from the Catalan parliament. This change gave new life to a separatist movement that had always existed in Catalonia, now bolstered by the region's economic success. On October 1, 2017, Catalonia held an independence referendum, which Spain's Constitutional Court declared illegal. Many people boycotted the election— only 43 percent voted, but of those who did, 90 percent wanted to become separate from Spain. Following a further vote in the Catalan parliament in Barcelona, Catalonia declared its independence.

For the first time in its history, Spain used emergency powers under its constitution to temporarily impose direct rule over Catalonia and dissolve the Catalan parliament. Many key leaders of the independence bid were jailed for sedition (inciting rebellion). Their attempt to break away from Spain had failed, but people continue to protest for independence and the centuries-long debate rumbles on.

Llibertat, Catalan for liberty
Hundreds of people in Barcelona protest against the trial of 12 imprisoned separatist leaders in February 2019, waving the Catalan flag.

> ## "In our changing world, nothing changes more than geography."
>
> **PEARL S. BUCK (1892–1973)**
> American writer and winner of the Nobel Prize in Literature

GEOPOLITICS is...

THE INFLUENCE OF GEOGRAPHICAL FACTORS, SUCH AS PHYSICAL TERRAIN, ON INTERNATIONAL RELATIONS AND POLITICS

SEE ALSO:

The term "geopolitics" was first coined by the Swedish political scientist Rudolf Kjellén in a book about Sweden's geography published in 1900. Today, geopolitics studies how nations' foreign policies and political behavior are explained by geographical features, such as climate, landscape, natural resources, and population. For example, the relations between different countries may be affected by a common geography, such as a shared water source, or the influence that resource-rich nations have on global politics.

SEA NATIONS

The late 19th- and early 20th-century American naval historian Alfred Thayer Mahan argued that control of the sea was politically and economically advantageous for a nation. It aided trade during peace time and naval military power during wars. One example was the rise of the British Empire during the 18th and 19th centuries. Great Britain was able to build a powerful navy and strong sea trade links partly because of its location in the Atlantic Ocean. Today, the economic power of China and Japan is helped by their access to the world's main shipping lanes.

LAND POWER

The invention of trains, cars, and trucks in the 1800s opened up nations at the heart of great land masses, such as Germany, and

huge nations like the US and Russia. Size matters in world politics. The vast, fertile farmlands, large rivers, and mineral resources of the US helped it to become the most powerful nation of the 1900s.

WATER

Access to fresh water for drinking and irrigating crops is essential for any country to survive. The Nile river rises in East Africa and flows north to Egypt and the Mediterranean Sea. Its basin covers 11 different countries. Efforts by countries upriver, such as Rwanda, Uganda, and Ethiopia to share the Nile's waters have been bitterly opposed by both Egypt and Sudan downstream. To avoid conflict, treaties have been put into place to manage water distribution. However, as water is becoming more scarce due to rising populations and climate change, there is increasing pressure on the region. Water scarcity is a concern in other parts of the world, too, such as China. Here, the government is introducing new technologies and modernizing the water infrastructure to try to combat the problem.

RAW MATERIALS

The political importance of a country often depends on its raw materials. The presence of vast oil and gas fields around the Persian Gulf gives countries in the region, such as Iran and Saudi Arabia, significant power in the world. Likewise, Turkey, which straddles

Europe and Asia, between the oil- and gas-rich Asian nations and energy-hungry nations of Europe, also holds considerable influence.

MODERN SILK ROAD

One attempt to redefine the geopolitics of Asia and Europe is China's "Belt and Road Initiative." This is a 21st-century successor to the ancient Silk Road that linked China to Europe 2,000 years ago. The new economic and strategic network aims, in the Chinese government's words, "to enhance regional connectivity and embrace a brighter future." The "Belt" is a series of roads and railroad lines connecting countries from China in the east to the Netherlands in the west. The "Road" is based on old maritime trade routes that linked countries around the Indian Ocean to the Mediterranean. Some observers of this vast project see it as an attempt by China to extend influence by building a Chinese-dominated trading network.

> "Mankind must put an end to war before war puts an end to mankind."

JOHN F. KENNEDY (1917-1963)
Former US president, addressing the UN General Assembly

WAR is...

ARMED CONFLICT BETWEEN STATES, GOVERNMENTS, MILITARY FORCES, OR OTHER POLITICAL GROUPS

Wars, whether they are between states or among peoples or groups of the same country, may break out over competition for territory or resources, or opposing religious or political beliefs. Borders between nations, races, and religions have often been established by wars.

WHY WAR?
Most countries in the world keep a standing army and other defense forces to protect their borders in case they are attacked. Some governments, however, have actively promoted the use of armed force as an instrument of national policy. This policy is known as "militarism." Militarism glorifies war, promotes heroism, and encourages patriotism. It is a feature of totalitarian dictatorships, but can also be an extension of imperialist and nationalist policies. The effect of war is catastrophic. With the advance of technology, the most destructive wars have taken place during the last century—in World War II (1939–1945) over 60 million people lost their lives.

NUCLEAR DETERRENT
After the end of World War II in 1945, a "Cold War" broke out between the capitalist West and the communist East. The Cold War was a tense rivalry, demonstrated by shows of military might and a nuclear "arms race" between the US and the Soviet Union. Direct combat between the two sides was avoided. However, the Cold War gave rise to the military policy of possessing nuclear weapons in order to deter other countries from attacking for fear of devastating retaliation. In 1968, more than 60 states signed a Non-Proliferation Treaty that aimed to reduce the spread of nuclear weapons.

peace. The Charter of the United Nations states that armed force can only be used in circumstances of self-defense or after approval from the UN Security Council. During the Korean War (1950–1953), the intervention of international forces to support South Korea's repulsion of a North Korean invasion, was sanctioned by the UN. In contrast, during the Vietnam War (1954–1975), warfare between the communist government of North Vietnam and its allies and the government of South Vietnam supported by the US, was not approved by the UN. It remains controversial today.

PACIFISM

Pacifism is the opposition to war and violence. Like many political ideas, pacifism can be interpreted in many ways. It may be based on moral principles of what is right and wrong, or on a pragmatic view that the costs of violence are so high that disputes must always be resolved peacefully. Absolute pacifists argue that the value of human life is such that there are never any circumstances in which war is justified. Conditional pacifists support the use of physical violence in the self-defense of themselves or others, or if their country is invaded. Selective pacifists draw a distinction between war, which they may not totally oppose, and the tools of warfare. They may support a conflict but be opposed to the use of weapons of mass destruction, be they nuclear, chemical, or biological. Conscientious objectors refuse to fight in wartime on the grounds of freedom of conscience. The Campaign for Nuclear Disarmament (CND), founded in the UK in 1957, actively campaigns for the abolition of nuclear and chemical weapons.

By 2016, 191 states had joined the Treaty, but some nations, such as India, Pakistan, and Israel have not signed it. North Korea withdrew from the agreement in 2003, and Iran has been sanctioned for breaking its terms.

ONLY IF NECESSARY

Wars and the use of military force are usually regarded as the result of a failure of politics or diplomacy to keep the peace. Today, the norms of what is acceptable in international behavior are known as international law. The United Nations (UN) organization, founded in 1945, is responsible for maintaining international

THE IRAQ WAR
2003

A US-led coalition of forces invaded Iraq on March 20, 2003. Its stated aims were to disarm the country and free the people from the repressive regime of Saddam Hussein. The US declared "mission accomplished" after 43 days, but the invasion has been widely condemned.

Saddam Hussein, a brutal dictator, had been president of Iraq since 1979. When his army invaded Iraq's oil-rich neighbor Kuwait in 1990, the United Nations (UN) backed a US-led military campaign to drive Iraq out. Iraq was defeated and, as a result, the UN directed it to destroy all its chemical, biological, and nuclear weapons of mass destruction (WMDs). Iraq, however, was reluctant to cooperate.

After the 9/11 terrorist attacks on New York in 2001, US foreign policy hardened. US President George W. Bush argued that Iraq's lack of compliance with UN weapons inspections posed a threat to the world. Then, in 2003, the UK published a dossier claiming that Iraq still had WMDs. This information was later comprehensively discredited.

In March 2003, without backing from the UN Security Council—and despite antiwar protests by millions of people worldwide—the US, UK, and other coalition forces invaded Iraq to oust Saddam. Fighting continued long after Bush had declared victory. A violent insurgency followed and over the next decade hundreds of thousands of Iraqi civilians were killed, injured, or lost their homes. The war and its aftermath sparked a heated international debate on the legality of foreign military interventions.

Toppling a tyrant
Saddam Hussein's statue is toppled as coalition forces take Baghdad in April 2003. Saddam himself was captured in December 2003, put on trial, and hanged in 2006.

"Saddam has gone,
but in his place we now
have 1,000 Saddams."

KADHIM AL-JABBOURI (born 1952)
An Iraqi who pulled down Saddam's statue, speaking in 2016
after years of political turmoil and civil war

> **"It has been said that arguing against globalization is like arguing against the laws of gravity."**
> KOFI ANNAN (1938–2018)
> Ghanaian diplomat, former UN secretary general, co-recipient of the Nobel Peace Prize

GLOBALIZATION is...

THE GROWING WEB OF INTERDEPENDENT GLOBAL CONNECTIONS BETWEEN PEOPLES, GOVERNMENTS, AND BUSINESSES

In the not too distant past, each country had its own economy, culture, and politics. Its industries were local and owned locally. It produced its own pop music and books, and its politicians were mainly concerned with local and national affairs. Each country had its own distinct character.

Today, many aspects of life are global in scope and impact, leading to a homogenization, or sameness, of life across the world. For instance, the fast-food chain McDonald's sells its burgers in more than 100 countries and they taste the same everywhere. Large companies operate around the globe, fashion, music, and movies cross borders, and transnational politics influence the world. This is known as "globalization."

SHRINKING THE WORLD
One of the first people to write about globalization was the sociologist Professor Roland Robertson. In 1992, he described globalization as "the compression of the world and the intensification of the consciousness of the world as a whole." In 2000, the International Monetary Fund, an organization that promotes financial cooperation between nations, said that there are four elements of globalization: trade and transactions, movement of capital and investment, migration of people, and the dissemination of knowledge. To these can now be added to the globalization of our environment through global warming, cross-boundary pollution, and the overfishing of the world's seas.

GLOBAL ECONOMY
The spread of international free trade and the development of modern international businesses in

the late 1900s created a global economy. Most dramatically, this new economy has been fueled by technological innovation, particularly the development of computers and the internet. The companies making the most profit all operate internationally. The five American hi-tech giants—Facebook, Apple, Amazon, Netflix, and Google—are so dominant they are known as "FAANG." Some global companies are worth more than the economies of nations, yet they are based in countries that impose relatively small taxes on businesses, so their tax bills are low while their profits remain high.

The services they provide are the same in every country, tying the world together in one big hi-tech "bundle."

POLITICAL IMPACT

Globalization has also made a big impact on politics. Economic freedom and the spread of ideas has led to liberal democracy now being the main form of government around the world. Some critics argue that globalization is leading to the death of national politics and the irrelevance of the state. However, there has also been a backlash against the formation of supranational unions (confederations made up of two or more nations), such as the European Union (EU). The decision of the UK to leave the EU, as voted for by the majority of the UK population in a 2016 referendum, was in part motivated by a desire to rebuild national sovereignty and uniqueness in the face of globalization.

EMBRACE OR RESIST?

Globalization has brought rising prosperity and technological advantages to some countries. It has enabled people to move between countries to take on higher-paying jobs. It has also engendered a cultural exchange, in which developed countries are increasingly influenced by the cultures of less developed nations—as well as the reverse, which was long the norm. But there are downsides. The practice of outsourcing services to lower-wage countries cuts costs for wealthier nations, but it also reduces the number of jobs in those wealthy nations and forces wages down there. Globalization's opponents also warn against the spread of capitalist attitudes, as opposed to community values, and the increasing income inequality caused by the movement of global capital.

ROHINGYA MIGRATION

AUGUST 2017

More people than ever before are living in countries that are not the land of their birth. Some migrants move to seek better economic opportunities, but many are fleeing from war, natural disasters, or persecution.

The Rohingya people, who are mostly Muslim, have lived in Myanmar for generations, but this mainly Buddhist country refuses them citizenship. In the face of discrimination and persecution over many decades, the Rohingya have been forced to flee their homes. In 2017, a Myanmar military operation killed thousands of Rohingya and triggered the exodus of more than 750,000 people into Bangladesh. The United Nations (UN) condemned it as ethnic cleansing (the forced removal of an ethnic or religious group from a region), one of the gravest crimes under international law.

These refugees—many starving and sick— fled on foot to take shelter in makeshift camps. The main camps are run by the UN with the Bangladeshi government, and are supported by aid agencies. They provide food, water, medicine, and basic education for children. However, the camps are overcrowded and vulnerable to disease, violence, and human trafficking (trade in people for forced labor).

Bangladesh is itself poor and overcrowded and its own people are at risk of displacement from rising sea levels and storms aggravated by climate change. Bangladeshi communities have welcomed the Rohingya, but the ongoing support of the refugees is a challenge.

Fleeing for their lives ▶
Rohingya refugees cross the Naf River from Myanmar into Bangladesh in October 2017. They are heading for refugee camps already overwhelmed with people in need.

"We want a guarantee of citizenship first and they must call us Rohingya, then we can go [back]."

RUHUL AMIN
A Rohingya refugee, speaking for his family of nine

> # "If we do not want to die together in war, we must learn to live together in peace."
> ### HARRY S. TRUMAN (1884–1972)
> Former US president, addressing the UN founding conference

INTERNATIONAL ORGANIZATIONS are...

INSTITUTIONS THAT PROMOTE AND SUPPORT COOPERATION AND UNDERSTANDING BETWEEN THE DIFFERENT STATES OF THE WORLD

International organizations are bodies set up between three or more states to tackle issues such as peace and security, trade, resources, and the environment. They are bound by treaties or other formal agreements and are usually governed by international law. Many work to improve people's lives throughout the world, regardless of their racial, religious, social, and national differences.

WORKING TOGETHER
One of the first global international organizations was the League of Nations, which was set up in 1920 after the horror of World War I. Its aim was to promote world peace and it established the fundamental idea that aggressive warfare is a crime. Without the membership of the US and other important states, the League failed and World War II broke out in 1939. However, it served as the model for the United Nations (UN), which was founded in 1945, and now has representatives from nearly every state in the world. The UN aims to maintain world peace and support human rights, the environment, and global economic development. Many international bodies, such as the World Health Organization (WHO) and United Nations Children's Fund (UNICEF), are specialist agencies of the UN. The WHO works to improve medical provision for all and reduce outbreaks of diseases such as Ebola, cholera, and HIV/AIDS.

REGIONAL ORGANIZATIONS

Not all organizations are global. The European Union (EU) brings together 27 European states into a political partnership and trading block, while the North Atlantic Treaty Organization (NATO) links 29 European and North American countries together in a defense partnership. Many other regional organizations exist around the world, some with an international outlook. The African Union (AU), for instance, promotes cooperation between 55 African states and protects African interests in international trade.

NONGOVERNMENTAL ORGANIZATIONS

A nongovernmental organization (NGO) is a body independent of any government that often operates on a not-for-profit, charitable basis. Many carry out humanitarian work and are able to work where national governments cannot, such as in war zones. The International Committee of the Red Cross (ICRC) was founded in Switzerland in 1863 to care for wounded soldiers on the battlefield. It is now governed by the four Geneva Conventions, rules that set out how soldiers and civilians should be treated in war. A more recent NGO, the Médecins Sans Frontières, founded in 1971 also provides medical care in war zones. Not all organizations are humanitarian in nature. The International Olympic Committee, for instance, aims to build a better world through sports.

WEAKNESSES

The differing ambitions of participating states can make it a challenge for an international organization to reach a consensus and take action. For instance, UN member states have struggled to agree on targets to counter climate change. The UN has long been criticized for being inefficient and spending too much money. Its powers are limited and its membership unbalanced and often divided. However, due in part to the peacekeeping initiatives of the UN, the number of deaths through war has declined since 1946 and fewer people are dying from famine today than in the 20th century.

DEMOCRACY IN THE U.S.

The United States is a federal republic: a group of states with an elected leader and elected representatives, in which every citizen has a say. The President, Congress, and the federal courts share in the governing of the nation, while state governments share sovereignty (or self-rule) with the federal government and have their own laws. This system is laid out in the U.S. Constitution which, unlike in some other countries, is an actual written document.

THE CONSTITUTION

Originally consisting of seven articles and drafted by James Madison, the Constitution became the supreme law in the U.S. in 1789. It defines the separation of powers, in which the federal government's three branches are defined.

The Bill of Rights

The first ten amendments, or additions to, the original Constitution are known as the Bill of Rights, and define important individual protections, such as the rights to free speech, a free press, and freedom of religion.

Amendments

The Constitution has been amended 17 subsequent times after the Bill of Rights. These amendments differ but generally expand individual liberty and specify how federal authority works.

Political parties

The United States political process is currently dominated by two main parties: the Democratic Party and the Republican Party. There are also much smaller parties, including the Green Party and the Libertarian Party. Other parties, such as the Whigs and Know-Nothings, have ceased to exist. U.S. citizens do not have to pick a political party to become candidates for election. They can register as Independent if they choose.

BRANCHES OF GOVERNMENT

The federal government of the United States is split into three branches: the Executive, Legislative, and Judicial. All are given equal power in the U.S. Constitution, and each has oversight power over the other two branches. Congress has further defined the duties and powers of each branch since the nation's beginning.

Executive

The elected President works with the Vice President and appoints a cabinet of secretaries to oversee governance.

Legislative

Better known as Congress, consisting of the Senate and the House of Representatives, it proposes and approves laws.

Judicial

The United States court system, which explains and applies the laws, culminates in the Supreme Court.

THE PRESIDENT

The United States President is the head of both state and the Government, as well as the nation's chief diplomat and leader of the Armed Forces. The President swears to protect and uphold the Constitution upon taking office. An election is held every four years to elect a President, and a President may serve no more than two terms.

State governments

Like the federal government, each of the 50 state governments splits power over its executive, legislative, and judicial branches. Each state has unique aspects to how laws work within its legal system, but all recognize themselves as part of the federal government in the U.S., which holds ultimate governmental authority.

CONGRESS

The two chambers of the U.S. Congress meet in the Capitol building in Washington, D.C., the nation's capital. Both senators and representatives are chosen through popular election, with each state's citizens selecting who will represent them.

Senate

There are 100 U.S. Senators. Each state, regardless of size or population, elects two senators to six-year terms. One-third of the Senate seats are up for election every two years.

House of Representatives

There are 435 Representatives. The number for each state is based on population, with one elected from each district. U.S. Representatives are elected for two-year terms.

THE SUPREME COURT

At the top of the Judicial branch is the Supreme Court, composed of nine justices, who are appointed for life by the President. One justice serves as the Chief Justice who oversees the business of the court. The justices represent a wide variety of political views, and rule on important cases that affect the nation.

ELECTIONS

In the United States, citizens vote to elect governmental leaders at the local, state, and federal levels. All citizens who are 18 years or older by Election Day and have registered can vote.

Presidential Elections for a new President are held every four years in November. Each party also has primary elections earlier in the year to choose its nominee. In many states only registered members of a political party may vote in a primary election.

Congressional Each state holds congressional elections every two years for Senators and Representatives.

State States hold elections to choose governors, state representatives and senators, and other officials who govern in the individual state.

Local Cities and counties have elections to choose city, county, and other local officials.

The Electoral College

While a general election is held for all voters in the United States, the President is not actually elected by the popular vote. Instead, each state sends electors equal to its representation in both houses of Congress to vote for the President as part of the Electoral College. There are 538 electors. A President must win 270 of those to take office.

DEMOCRACY IN CANADA

As a former colony of Great Britain, Canada's political system is based on that of the United Kingdom. It is a parliamentary democracy set within a constitutional monarchy, composed of three parts: the Queen of Canada as head of state (represented in Canada by the Governor General at the federal level or a lieutenant-governor at the provincial level), the Senate, and the House of Commons. The Queen holds a mostly ceremonial role.

THE CONSTITUTION

Canada's Constitution consists of a large collection of documents that set out the country's governing legal framework, including the structure of Parliament, the election process, and the role of the Monarchy.

PARLIAMENTARY DEMOCRACY

In Canada, the citizens elect the people who govern them, known as Members of Parliament (MPs) in the federal government. MPs serve in Parliament, where they propose new bills, debate, and represent their constituents.

ELECTIONS

Canadian voters elect people to a variety of different governmental positions, including MPs who represent them in the federal government, Members of Provincial Parliament (MPPs), and local councilors and other officials who take care of local issues. All Canadian citizens 18 years and older who have registered can vote in elections.

General elections

General elections are held every four years to elect MPs to the House of Commons. The leader of the party with the most MPs becomes Prime Minister and forms the government. General elections use a First Past the Post voting system.

Electoral districts

Canada is divided into federal electoral districts, or ridings, based on population. The residents of each riding vote to elect an MP to represent them. There are also electoral districts for provincial and territorial elections.

GOVERNMENT IN CANADA

In Canada's parliamentary democracy, there are three levels of government: federal, provincial or territorial, and municipal. The federal government, headed by the elected Prime Minister, is split into three branches: Executive, Legislative, and Judicial. Together, the Executive and the Legislative branches form the Parliament and work to create federal laws, policies, and regulations in Canada. The Judicial branch is in charge of interpreting the laws made by Parliament, as well as deciding if laws have been broken. The Judicial branch is kept separate from Parliament to ensure that it remains unbiased and independent.

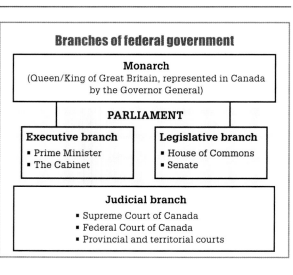

Executive branch

The Prime Minister and his or her Cabinet form the Executive branch. Cabinet members are chosen by the PM to help manage the government, with each Cabinet Minister overseeing a specific department, such as health care, foreign affairs, and national defense.

Legislative branch

This branch of the government consists of two parts, the House of Commons and the Senate, who work together to create new laws or amend existing ones. For a bill to become law, it must be approved by both the House and the Senate.

HOUSE OF COMMONS

The House of Commons has 338 seats, held by elected MPs. The political party that wins the most seats in the House will form the new Government, with its leader as Prime Minister. The party with the second largest number of seats forms the Official Opposition. MPs hold their seats until the government is dissolved. Most laws begin as bills proposed in the House of Commons.

SENATE

The Senate has 105 seats. Senators are appointed by the Governor General and may serve until the age of 75. Senators study, amend, and either approve or reject bills passed by the House of Commons. The Senate can also introduce bills of their own, with certain restrictions.

Role of the Governor General

The Governor General represents the Queen in Canada and is responsible for duties such as swearing in a new Prime Minister, opening and dissolving sessions of Parliament, giving royal assent to new laws passed by the House and the Senate, appointing new members of the Senate, and serving as Commander-in-Chief of Canada's armed forces.

MAJORITY VS MINORITY GOVERNMENT

If a political party with the most candidates elected to the House of Commons wins more than half of the seats, it forms a majority government. If it wins less than half the seats, it forms a minority government. Majority governments are more powerful than minority governments, as they have enough members in the House to win any vote. A minority government may join forces with one of the smaller opposition parties to form a coalition government in order to control the majority of the seats in the House, but this has been rare in Canadian history.

POLITICAL PARTIES

All political parties in Canada are based on key ideas and principles that members feel are particularly important, such as education and health care. In Canada, there are three main political parties: the Liberal Party of Canada, the Conservative Party of Canada, and the New Democratic Party. There are also smaller and regional parties, such as the Green Party and the Bloc Québécois, as well as independent candidates with no party affiliation.

Seats in the House after October 2019 federal election

Liberal Party of Canada	157
Conservative Party of Canada	121
Bloc Québécois	32
New Democratic Party	24
Green Party	3
Independent	1

The Liberals form a minority government with the Conservatives as the Official Opposition.

GLOSSARY

-archy/-cracy
A word ending in -archy or -cracy describes a type of government, such as monarchy or democracy.

-ism
A word ending in -ism is a name given to a specific set of political ideas, or ideologies, for example capitalism, or other beliefs, such as feminism.

absolutism
A style of government in which one person or one political group has complete control over everything.

advocate
Someone who publicly recommends a particular policy or action.

assimilation
The process by which people whose ethnic origins and cultures are different from the majority gradually take on many of the characteristics of the dominant group.

austerity
A set of measures brought in by a government to reduce its budget shortfall. Such measures involve cuts in public spending and increases in taxation.

authoritarianism
Inflexible control by a government which restricts people's rights and freedoms.

authority
The right or power to impose rules on someone else.

autocracy
A form of government in which one person or group holds total power.

autonomy
The right of a state or territory to be self-governing.

ballot
A system used to select candidates in an election, under which people cast their votes in secret.

bias
A strong preference for or prejudice against something. The term is often used in relation to the media, which is seen to lean toward one political viewpoint or another.

bourgeoisie
The social group that largely comprises middle-class capitalists.

capital
Financial or other assets such as land or buildings.

citizen
A person who legally belongs to a particular country and is entitled to its rights and protection.

civic
Relating to a city and the people who live there.

civil
Relating to the ordinary people of a country who are not connected to military or religious organizations.

civil disobedience
A nonviolent refusal to obey the laws made by government.

civil society
The sector of society that includes organizations such as businesses and charities, and operates for public benefit but is not part of government.

class system
The organization of people into groups that indicate their status in a society, such as middle or working class.

coalition
In government, a temporary alliance of different political parties, usually when no party has gained a majority in an election.

confederation
An alliance of different groups of people who work together to achieve common political aims but retain most of the control of their own areas.

Congress
The lawmaking branch of the US government, made up of elected politicians. The duties of Congress include monitoring government practice and approving public spending.

constitutionalism
The form of government that follows a constitution: the written laws and principles of a country.

corruption
The dishonest or criminal use of power for either private or political gain.

culture
The customs, behavior, and social norms of a country or society.

deregulation
The removal of government control from a business or industry.

despot
A ruler who holds absolute power and uses it to oppress or terrorize the people.

diplomacy
The art of conducting international negotiations between governments and their representatives.

dissemination
The spreading of information.

dystopia
An imaginary society of the future in which there is typically some form of total control over an oppressed people.

egalitarianism
The belief that all people are equal socially, politically, and economically.

elitism
The belief that society should be governed by those people who possess the greatest wealth, power, and privilege.

Enlightenment, the
A period of intellectual development in 18th-century Europe, when thinkers questioned long-established ideas on religion and tried to find new ways of reasoning.

ethical
Conforming to standards of morally and legally acceptable behavior.

executive
The branch of government responsible for seeing that laws and policies are carried out.

extremism
The holding of extreme political or religious opinions, especially those that condone the use of violence.

federation
A system of government, as seen in the USA, where a group of authorities makes the rules of state but retain power over their own local areas.

fiscal policy
The way in which a government adjusts taxation and public spending to influence a country's economic conditions.

franchise
In political terms, the right to vote in an election.

free market
A form of economy that is controlled by supply and demand, without government involvement.

fundamentalism
The strict observance of a religion or set of political beliefs that does not allow any differing opinions.

government
The political control of a state or society; also, the group of people who exercise that control.

guerrilla warfare
War waged by small groups of independent civilian fighters against regular armed forces. Guerrilla tactics include ambush, surprise raids, and propaganda.

harassment
Unwanted and uninvited behavior that makes someone feel intimidated, threatened, or offended.

head of government
The leader of a government, who holds the most political power and authority.

head of state
The leading representative of a state, who often holds a mainly symbolic role and is sometimes also the head of government. Usually either a president or monarch.

ideology
The ideas and convictions that form the basis of a group's beliefs. Political ideologies include socialism, liberalism, and conservatism.

illiberal
Being opposed to the belief that people should have freedom of choice and speech.

illiberal democracy
A political system in which the government is elected by the people but restricts their freedom and blocks the spread of information about its actions.

inalienable
In politics, an inalienable right is one that cannot be given away or transferred.

independence
The freedom of a country, state, or society to be self-governing. An independent politician is one who runs for office while not identifying with any specific political party.

interest group
A formal group of people or organizations that attempts to achieve its own ends by pressuring a government to change policy.

judiciary
The branch of government that is responsible for administering justice and which includes courts of law.

laissez-faire
The term is taken from the French, meaning "to leave alone." It is used to describe one of the theories of capitalism—that an economic system works best without government interference.

left wing
Sympathetic to socialist, liberal, or communist aims and ideologies.

legislature
The group of people charged with making the laws for a state or city.

liberal democracy
A form of democratic government in which political power is limited by law, and people's rights and freedoms are protected.

libertarianism
The theory that there should be greater freedom in a society for its citizens, and less government control.

lobby
To attempt to convince someone with political influence that a situation or piece of legislation should be changed.

mandate
Authorization to do something. In politics, a mandate is a formal instruction from an electorate to their government representative.

Maoism
A variation of Marxism–Leninism associated with the politics and teachings of Mao Zedong, Chairman of the Communist Party of China from 1949 to 1976.

martial law
Military control that replaces the normal civilian government of a country, usually to maintain order in times of crisis.

Marxism–Leninism
A variation on Marxist theory that was formulated by the Russian revolutionary and politician Lenin (1870–1924), and became the ideology of the Communist Party of the Soviet Union.

means of production
In Marxist theory, these are the resources, such as factories, machinery, and materials, that are needed to produce goods and services, as well as the labor that uses them.

monetarism
The theory that a government can create a stable economy by controlling the supply of money.

nationalization
The takover of private businesses or industries by the government to bring them under state control.

nation-state
An independent state in which the majority of the citizens share a common language and culture.

nominal
Existing in name only. For instance, a nominal president may be called a president but does not have full presidential powers or duties.

parliament
The lawmaking branch of a country's government, often made up of elected politicians. The duties of a parliament include monitoring government practice and approving public spending.

patriarchy
A social system in which men are dominant over women, holding all the political power and having exclusive control of finances and property.

platform
The published statement of a political party's aims and intentions.

political party
An organized group of people who share the same political opinions and aim to achieve political power through their chosen representatives.

pragmatism
One of the key ideas of conservatism: that decision-making should be a flexible process, based on practical considerations and not on theories.

president
The leader of a republican state, usually elected by the people.

pressure group
People with a common interest who join together to persuade those in power to support their cause.

prime minister
The leader of the political party that is in government.

privatization
Moving a government-run service or industry, such as healthcare or transportation, into private ownership.

proletariat
In Marxist theory, the working classes.

propaganda
Information spread to promote a cause, always heavily biased toward one set of opinions and often misleading.

racism
Prejudice and discrimination against people because of a belief that their race makes them somehow inferior.

radicalism
The belief that extreme measures are justified in bringing about changes in society.

reactionary
Opposing social or political change or reform.

referendum
A vote offered to the general electorate for them to decide on a proposed political action.

reform
In politics, an amendment made to a practice or law in order to improve it.

representation
The process of speaking on behalf of or acting for someone else. A politician may represent, or act on behalf of, a group of people.

republicanism
The theory that a republic, ideally a state led by a democratically elected head, is a better form of government than a monarchy. In the US, the term means support for the Republican Party or GOP (Grand Old Party).

right wing
Sympathetic to conservative or reactionary aims and ideologies.

rule of law
The concept that all members of society, both private individuals and those serving in government, are subject to fair and just laws.

sectarianism
Strong support for a particular political or religious group.

secularism
The belief that religion should be kept separate from political activities and the everyday affairs of society.

sexism
Discrimination or prejudice against someone because of their gender.

social contract
A contract between the members of a society and their government agreeing on the policies and laws that are acceptable on both sides.

society
The people who make up an organized community within a region or state and interact with each other on a regular basis.

sovereign
A ruler with the greatest authority and power in a country.

sovereignty
The authority held by the ruler of a state that is not subject to any outside control or influences.

Soviet Union
Another name for the USSR.

state
A political region and the people who live in it, under the leadership of a ruler who may, or may not, have been democratically elected.

strategy
A plan to achieve one or more goals.

supply and demand
The balance between the amount of goods available and the number of people who want to buy the products.

tax
A compulsory payment to the government, based on income and assets, which is used to finance public services such as education, the police, and road maintenance.

tyranny
A government in which one person takes control in his or her own interests rather than for the general good.

unethical
Not morally or legally acceptable.

USSR
The Union of Soviet Socialist Republics: from 1922 to 1991, the name given to the confederation of socialist states that replaced the former tzarist Russian Empire.

utopia
An imagined society in which everything is perfect, with just laws, fair and honest government, and ideal lifestyles for all citizens.

INDEX

Page numbers in **bold** refer to main entries.

ACKNOWLEDGMENTS

Dorling Kindersley would like to thank Steve Crozier for creative retouching, Louise Stevenson for editorial assistance, Caroline Stamps for proofreading, and Helen Peters for the index.

The publisher would like to thank the following for their kind permission to reproduce their photographs:

(Key: a-above; b-below/bottom; c-center; f-far; l-left; r-right; t-top)

12-13 Alamy Stock Photo: PNC Collection. **18-19** Getty Images: Heritage Images. **22-23** Getty Images: Alain Dejean. **28-29** Alamy Stock Photo: dpa picture alliance. **34** Getty Images: Media24 / Gallo Images (t). **35** Alamy Stock Photo: Oistein Thomassen. **38** Alamy Stock Photo: Zoonar GmbH. **44** Alamy Stock Photo: Shawshots (t). **45** Alamy Stock Photo: Photo 12. **48-49** Getty Images: Bettmann. **54-55** Getty Images: Tom Stoddart Archive.

62-63 Getty Images: Print Collector. **66-67** Getty Images: NurPhoto. **68-69** Getty Images: Ulrich Baumgarten. **74-75** Alamy Stock Photo: WDC Photos. **78-79** Getty Images: Don Cravens. **86-87** Shutterstock: Jaipal Singh / EPA-EFE. **90** Alamy Stock Photo: GL Archive (t). **91** Alamy Stock Photo: Niday Picture Library. **96-97** Getty Images: SOPA Images. **106** Getty Images: AFP (t). **107** Alamy Stock Photo: Alpha Historica. **110-111** Getty Images: Sergei Supinsky. **114-115** Getty Images: Jimmy Sime. **122-123** Getty Images: Jonathan Rashad. **124** Getty Images: bjdlzx. **130** Getty Images: (t). **131** Getty Images: Dinodia Photos. **134-135** Getty Images: Lluis Gene. **140-141** Getty Images: Robert Nickelsberg. **144-145** Getty Images: Fred Dufour.

All other images © Dorling Kindersley

For further information see: **www.dkimages.com**